99 TACTICS FOR SUCCESS

Enjoy this life! ~ Dr. Carrie

SELF HELP
ON THE GO

Because You Are Not Broken,
But Life Gets Tricky Sometimes

Dr. Carrie Johansson

© 2022 by Dr. Carrie Johansson
All rights reserved.
Printed in the United States of America.

No part of this publication may be reproduced or distributed in any form or by any means, without the prior permission of the publisher. Requests for permission should be directed to permissions@indiebooksintl.com, or mailed to Permissions, Indie Books International, 2424 Vista Way, Suite 316, Oceanside, CA 92054.

The views and opinions in this book are those of the author at the time of writing this book, and do not reflect the opinions of Indie Books International or its editors.

Neither the publisher nor the author is engaged in rendering legal or other professional services through this book. If expert assistance is required, the services of appropriate professionals should be sought. The publisher and the author shall have neither liability nor responsibility to any person or entity with respect to any loss or damage caused directly or indirectly by the information in this publication.

Stories In This Book

All stories in this book are based on true events, but names and details have been changed to maintain patient confidentiality. The purpose of the stories is educational, so you can better understand the tactics in action.

ISBN-13: 978-1-952233-86-9
Library of Congress Control Number: 2021923448

Designed by SP Book Design
INDIE BOOKS INTERNATIONAL®, INC.
2424 VISTA WAY, SUITE 316
OCEANSIDE, CA 92054
www.indiebooksintl.com

CONTENTS

Preface..................................v

PART I: FEEL BETTER..........................1
  Chapter 1: Calm Your Nerves 3
  Chapter 2: Beat The Blues....................25
  Chapter 3: Knock Out Anger..................47

PART II: FIND YOUR CENTER.................69
  Chapter 4: Lighten Up 71
  Chapter 5: Feel Happier Today................93
  Chapter 6: Get Your Point Across 117
  Chapter 7: Survive Sticky Situations..........137

PART III: MOVE FORWARD 161
  Chapter 8: Enhance Relationships............163
  Chapter 9: De-Stress 187
  Chapter 10: Live The Life You Want..........209

Appendix................................233
  Acknowledgments 233
  About The Author 235
  Works Referenced........................237

PREFACE

Having a tough day? Feeling totally stressed out? Want quick, easy-to-apply solutions to your issues that really work? Unlike your typical self-help book that takes significant time and effort to work through, this book is laid out as my clients told me they wanted it to be: with multiple suggestions for life's most common problems, using research-based techniques tested by real people.

This is a different kind of book. This is a human owner's manual, designed for you, the ambitious, overworked human with a lot going on. It is a book of tactics, ranging from light and easy suggestions to "going deeper" tips that take a little more time and attention. All of them, however, are designed to be helpful in and of themselves. You should be able to pick up this book, turn to a section or a chapter, and thumb through until you find something helpful to you, likely something helpful *in the very moment* you read it. The tips are written to be easy to understand, inexpensive, effective, and simple to apply. These are my favorite ninety-nine suggestions, the ones I use all the time in my practice, the tips my clients say really, really work.

This book is based on a simple principle with a fancy name: psychological flexibility. Psychological flexibility means you are in the present moment, accepting reality as it is and then asking yourself: What's my next best move?

We can learn to help our minds become more helpful, flexible, and efficient, or we can succumb to the power of old, unhelpful habits that make our brains progressively more stuck. Here I offer ninety-nine ways to help use the power of psychological flexibility so you can build resiliency and change your habitual way of responding to life's most common problems. For good. Life, unfortunately, will continue to be stressful, but as you approach reality with less resistance and use your core values to make choices, you'll find yourself working through issues more easily, with less wear and tear on your psyche.

Since you probably have to manage more than one emotion, problem, or troublesome situation in a day, this book covers the top problem areas most people experience in a typical busy life. The first section focuses on emotions, the second section on general principles about how to keep yourself functioning well despite life's day-to-day challenges, and finally, the last section helps you move forward in your life.

Check out this preview of the contents:

PART I: FEEL BETTER

We all have a wide range of emotions to field on a day-to-day basis. The top three we often describe as "negative" emotions are anxiety, sadness, and anger. Here we are offering you a new definition of feeling better. Instead of stuffing, ignoring, or acting out your negative emotions, we are going to teach you how to manage them more effectively.

CHAPTER 1: CALM YOUR NERVES

Welcome to Wrangling Anxiety 101. Start here to learn how to settle down your mind, calm your body, decrease fear, and get control over worry.

CHAPTER 2: BEAT THE BLUES

What to do when life gets you down. Sadness is part of the human experience. Here are some tips to help you set aside the sadness when you're feeling low.

CHAPTER 3: KNOCK OUT ANGER

Beat up on anger before it beats up on you. Anger often feels out of control, but it does serve a purpose and can be managed. Here are some tips that can help.

Preface

PART II: FIND YOUR CENTER

Able to manage your emotions already? Awesome. Let's better understand ourselves and how we interact with the world. This section gives you great information on how to soften your mood, increase happiness, communicate better, and successfully navigate some of life's typical curveballs.

CHAPTER 4: LIGHTEN UP

What the funk? Sometimes things just feel off, and we don't know quite what to do. Here are some tips to skillfully manage the mixture of emotions life can bring.

CHAPTER 5: FEEL HAPPIER TODAY

Get happy: Happiness researchers suggest that we are in charge of about 40 percent of our happiness, with 10 percent determined by external events and the other 50 percent predetermined by genetics and upbringing. Here are some tips to maximize your 40 percent.[1]

CHAPTER 6: GET YOUR POINT ACROSS

Speak up. Communication is critical but often not so easy. Here are some tips to get you on the right track when you're talking to those other pesky humans.

CHAPTER 7: SURVIVE STICKY SITUATIONS

Welcome to Daily Hassles 102. Life typically presents us with a variety of challenges, ranging from the very small to the very large. Here are some suggestions about how to change the sticky situations of life from problems into opportunities.

PART III: MOVE FORWARD

Now onto the juicy stuff, tips on how to really enjoy yourself. Here we discuss some of the best bits of life, but also the same bits that can send us sliding sideways when they aren't going well: relationships, stress, and life purpose questions.

CHAPTER 8: ENHANCE RELATIONSHIPS

The joy of connection: At the end of the day, relationships are what give most people a strong motivation to enjoy this awesome planet of ours. Here are some tips to make them feel good.

CHAPTER 9: DE-STRESS

Welcome to Stress 103: Managing life's inevitable stressors is critical for your physical and mental health. Here are some tips to help you stress less.

CHAPTER 10: LIVE THE LIFE YOU WANT

Reset your barometer for success: Healthy, enriching relationships, enjoyable activities, meaningful work, and an emphasis on living your best life systematically improves your overall well-being.

> *Feel free to read this book in order or turn immediately to the section that best describes what you are struggling with.*

Pick it up as you need it, and enjoy relief quickly, with in-the-moment lessons we know really work.

This book is designed for folks who are basically mentally healthy who want to discover more information about how to become their best selves. If you are someone with serious or persistent mental health issues, this book would be like putting a Band-Aid on a geyser. Don't fret; even major mental health issues are treatable, just not by this book or any book. If you are struggling with these types of issues, please seek the in-person assistance of a trained, licensed therapist, doctor, or clinic. This book should not be used as a substitute for therapy or medical advice.

Dr. Carrie Johansson

PART I

FEEL BETTER

ONE OF THE major causes of stress for us humans is the experience of emotions, particularly the "negative" emotions such as anxiety, sadness, and anger. We tend to resist these strong emotions and treat them like they are bad. This section gives you expert information on how to understand and manage emotions instead of either reacting explosively or stuffing them away. Let's improve our skills and make things that ordinarily feel complex easier to manage. The better we can understand, accept, and handle our emotional world, the easier life becomes. Let's change those patterns of over-reacting and feeling overwhelmed by emotions and instead skillfully respond to our feelings.

How many times have you been upset and been told to "calm down"? (This, by the way, is incredibly ineffective. Never in the history of increased calmness has this been achieved by the order to "calm down.") We tell people, "Don't be scared," or the equally unhelpful, "Don't be mad." We say, "Stop freaking out," or ask them, "Why are you so negative?" We have an entire cultural narrative supporting the suppression of *all* negative emotions. It is so dominant that even people who love us will be insistent that we should get out of our bad mood as quickly as possible and return to feeling happy ASAP.

I hate to be the bearer of bad news, but emotions are just emotions. We have a wide range of them, and they come up whether we want them to or not. Some of them are certainly more fun than others, like: Joy. Success. Love. Others are less enjoyable, like grief, rage, or fear. They aren't, however, technically good or bad, positive or negative. All emotions are transient (even if the less enjoyable ones feel like they are going to last forever), and all emotions work best when recognized, acknowledged, and processed. Instead of attempting to stop feeling bad and to begin to feel good (instantaneously), how about we teach you how to manage the range of emotions that will inevitably arise?

Emotion needs to be recognized and moved through instead of pushed aside, suppressed, or replaced by trying to pile on positives. What a relief it can be to understand that it is normal to have a range of emotions and to know how to better tolerate uncomfortable emotional experiences. We are not robots; we are supposed to have an uneven experience of the world. Sometimes happy, sometimes, well, not so much. So, when you're in that "not so much" stage of things, here are suggestions to help.

CHAPTER 1:
CALM YOUR NERVES

TACTIC #1
START BY FEELING SAFE

THIS IS A building block at its most basic. If you're not safe, nothing else feels okay. One of the first things I do as a therapist is to check in with clients about safety in their lives. I am especially motivated to do this with clients who are complaining about anxiety, and I make it a must for folks who have a history of trauma. Safety is critical because it represents the opposite of a sense of fear. An impending sense of doom or persistent worry about what might happen next is typical for someone complaining about anxiety symptoms and is a hallmark symptom after trauma.

Safety is something you can feel in both your physical body as well as your mental/emotional states. Safety comes up in relationships and with life tasks like managing money. Let's start by looking at safety in your external environment—you know, like your home, work, and general life.

APPLY THIS: Look around your life right this minute. Is there one small thing you can do to feel just a little safer in the moment? Read through the safety checklist and see how many of these might apply to you. Don't worry; different things will resonate with different people. These are some ideas to improve your sense of external safety and eliminate unnecessary worries.

SAFETY CHECKLIST:

HOUSE BASICS:
- Lock your doors and windows.
- Have operational fire alarms and keep a fire extinguisher handy.
- Lock up firearms, especially in homes with small children.
- Have candles, matches, water, and snacks in your pantry for power outages.
- Keep your home's exterior well lit.

CAR BASICS:
- Lock your doors when driving.
- Wear your seat belt.
- Park where there is good lighting.
- Never drive impaired (drunk, stoned, overtired).
- Tuck your valuables out of sight when you leave your car.

PERSONAL BASICS:
- Seat yourself in public places with your back supported and face the entrance.
- Minimize contact with or eliminate toxic people from your life.
- If you drink or use drugs, always keep yourself from total impairment.
- Use a buddy system when you hike, bike, or explore new places.
- Never leave your drink unattended when out at a bar or a restaurant.
- Have a financial cushion in your checking account (even if it is just $100).
- On a first date, always meet the person in a public location.
- While in crowded places, notice where the nearest exit is in case of emergency.

TACTIC #2
BREATHE INTO YOUR TENSE BODY

After increasing safety in our external environment, it is important to attend to our internal environment. Our bodies hold tension as a response to feeling unsafe. Remember that sketchy-looking guy who crowded you on the subway? Yeah, I bet your whole body tensed right up, even if he was harmless.

When our bodies are tense, it tells our brains that we are unsafe. When you relax your body, it sends a memo to your brain that you're safe and sound. Maybe you feel a tight sensation in your chest or churning in your stomach, maybe your neck is flushed, or your shoulders are tight. Settling down your physiology is one of the easiest and best ways to decrease these anxious feelings and increase your ability to logically think through what is going on. Here are instructions for progressive relaxation.

APPLY THIS: Read through this first, then close your eyes and work through the steps.

Start in a comfortable position, maybe sitting in a comfy chair or lying down on a couch. Uncross your legs and arms. Try to straighten yourself up so you are nicely aligned. Now imagine starting at the top of your head and relaxing your scalp. Loosen the connection between your head and neck by moving your head gently from side to side. Imagine your face softening and relax your tongue (always the hardest part for me). Relax your shoulders away from your ears, maybe roll them once or twice to work out the kinks and imagine the tension in your back melting away.

Imagine breathing calm into your body with every in-breath and releasing tension with every out-breath. Imagine that the tension flows out of your toes and fingers, and everything you release dissolves as soon as it hits the air.

Go down your back, progressively relaxing as you descend through your spine. Come back up and go down your chest and arms, imagining everything getting looser, more relaxed, and more comfortable with every breath. Descend into your hips and thighs, releasing tension and discomfort. Imagine your knees feeling lubricated and flexible. Imagine your calves being totally relaxed. Let your ankles loosen, and your feet feel less cramped and tense. Spread out your toes and flex and relax your feet.

Now breathe throughout your body and notice any leftover areas of tension. Imagine cushioning those areas with gentle warmth and care, just noticing they are still there. Don't fret if every single part isn't totally relaxed. The point here is to relax your body more than it was when you first started this process. Breathe in calm a few more times and then bring yourself back into the room. This gets you into your body in the present moment. Good? Repeat often.

PS: This is an especially effective way to relax before going to bed.

TACTIC #3
IMAGINE THE BEST-CASE SCENARIO

Feeling worried? I bet your brain is spinning all sorts of tales about what awful things could come true, about life being ruined, or someone getting hurt, about failing something, or letting someone down. A hallmark of anxious thinking is focusing on what *isn't* going to go well. We don't typically get anxious about something going right, although some folks get worked up about succeeding, creating a whole new set of worries. I particularly love to work with people who put themselves in a double bind, simultaneously thinking: "Yikes, what if I fail?" and "Oh no, what will it mean if I succeed?"

Worst-case scenario thinking helps fuel and feed our anxious thoughts. It isn't typically helpful in moments of crisis because we tend to be incredibly terrible at predicting the future. Most of the time, our worst-case imaginings don't bear much resemblance to the hard things we have to face in reality.

You can stop yourself from thinking that you are going to ruin your life or your job, or that someone is going to get hurt, or that a loved one is going to die, or whatever else your mind is trying to focus on that is a worst-case scenario because none of it is likely to happen in the next little bit of time. Let's take those illogical thoughts by the horns and redirect them in a more helpful direction.

TWO THINGS TO APPLY: First, see if what you are worried about is something within your control. Think through what you can do to feel safe and get prepared. For example, if you are going backpacking, you can anticipate what you realistically need for the trip and prepare for things that otherwise you would worry about. So, yes, bring your bear spray, bug spray, waterproof matches, sleeping bag, and sunscreen. Have some information about how to make a shelter and take a map with you. *Think through* your needs and do what you can to prepare yourself so you can feel good about going.

Second, you can move beyond preparation and work with your mindset by expanding your thinking past worst-case scenarios to include more realistic possibilities.

Let's say you are working on a project for work, and you've started imagining that you won't meet your deadline and will be shamed publicly for it in a board meeting, and next, you will be fired. Okay, stop yourself right there. What do you need to do to prepare so you can get things done well, on time? Get that taken care of first. Then, take yourself through a visual of getting the project complete, presenting it well, and getting a compliment on your work. Notice that I am not suggesting that you imagine winning employee of the year. Neither the scenario of getting fired or winning employee of the year are helpful. Instead, the goal is to imagine a balanced image of a positive outcome and enjoy the relief from the worst-case scenario.

TACTIC #4
USE A STOP SIGN

Several years ago, I was prepping to go on a reunion trip with my high school friends. I was super excited to go and be with ladies I hadn't seen, some in over twenty-five years (let's just say high school was a while ago for me). Rather than staying in that excitement, however, I got panicked that the trip would go badly, that I wasn't good enough, or I'd be the person who had made the most life mistakes. I got stuck packing because I was hung up on trying to look perfect. I started wondering if I should even go at all since I was feeling so lousy. I called one of my best friends who was also going on the trip and confessed my thoughts. She laughed and said, "You too? I thought I was the only one thinking all negative." We shared a laugh, assured each other that the trip wasn't about judgment, and ended up going and having a blast.

The anxiety I was experiencing, while silly on the surface, was really spinning me around. That is one of the tough things about anxiety: nervous thoughts seem to take on a mind of their own and take you to nasty places that make things worse. However, when you try to push the anxiety away, it tends to gain strength. Let's stop this terrible pattern.

APPLY THIS:

> S: Stop the spinning
> T: Think
> O: review Options
> P: Proceed forward

First, *Stop* the spinning. Visualize a huge, red stop sign, hear the word "STOP" in your mind, see "STOP" flash bright red in front of your eyes. Imagine being in a car and feeling your body move against the seatbelt as you come to a stop. Use your visual, auditory (hearing), and/or tactile senses to activate your brain into stopping.

Next, choose to *Think* about what is going on inside your mind. What are your thoughts trying to say? Is there any truth to them? (If you are walking down a dark alley and you feel scared, maybe this *is* a feeling you should listen to.) Investigate the source of the spinning thoughts and examine how realistic they are. Once you understand the thoughts better, you'll have more choices concerning thought management.

Third, review your *Options*. Anything you can do to calm down? Anything you need to do differently, either in your actions and behaviors or in your mind? What choices do you have in this moment, right now? Worried you don't have any good choices? Then try to buy yourself some time until you can make a more reasoned choice.

Finally, *Proceed* forward with a reasoned plan. Notice how the plan makes you feel. Breathe into your body to decrease tension. Notice your thoughts. Ask yourself what the most helpful move would be. If you are still spinning, imagine you are a scientist trying to get to the bottom of a curious behavior: Examine what is at the root of the thoughts and what you can do differently. Repeat until you can get a solid plan and move in a good direction.

TACTIC #5

DRINK A GLASS OF WATER (UPSIDE DOWN IF YOU MUST)

Feeling out of control with worry? Starting to sweat about something coming up? Is your mind going into that horrible negative spiral of fear and concern? Let's introduce a quick distraction and get your brain derailed from its collision course with fear and dread.

When I was a kid, I would get hiccups with some frequency. It was annoying and uncomfortable. I would start to worry that the hiccups would last all day (the all-day hiccups *did* happen to me a few times, setting the stage for that fear to grow). My mom knew all the typical tricks everyone said worked to cure the hiccups, but these didn't work so well for me: The teaspoon of sugar was delicious but ineffective; scaring me just, well, scared me. What did work, however, was trying to drink a glass of water upside down. Not only did this work pretty darn well at eliminating the hiccups, more importantly, it also took my mind off the problem and effectively focused my attention on the moment.

Now, if you have ever tried to drink a glass of water upside down, you know it is tricky business. You have to bend over, tip your head upside down, and drink from the opposite side of the glass. If you don't focus, the water goes all over you. If you do focus, however, it seems to circumvent the hiccups and gets your body back to normal. It is extremely difficult to be fully engaged (meaning no spills) in drinking your water upside down and be thinking about anything else. This keeps you from feeling anxious or from fretting about *anything* except keeping the water in the glass and going directly into your mouth.

Notice that this little exercise takes you away from a negative feeling (worry) and puts you squarely into a productive activity (drinking). It does so without you needing to bully yourself into feeling something different, without any self-criticism about your emotions, without any effort at all in terms of changing emotions. *The emotions change simply because you have shifted your focus to productive action in the present moment.*

APPLY THIS: Try the drinking-water-upside-down trick, or whatever works for you as a quick distraction, a break from the emotion, helping you distance from the worry. Get engaged in the present moment with a simple activity. Ideally, your activity should be something non-harmful and easy to do. Sometimes a simple shift in focus can work wonders.

TACTIC #6
CONTROL SOMETHING SMALL

WORRY TENDS TO leave people feeling out of control. It is one of the defining features of the emotion: Feeling out of control, like something awful is going to happen and you can't make it not happen. You don't feel in charge. You're not feeling like the master of your own destiny. This is pretty uncomfortable stuff, especially when your mind starts down the path of things you have no control over at that moment. For example, you find yourself worrying that your preschool child eventually won't get into college or worrying that you will be fired when the management at your office changes six months from now, or you are panicked that you will eventually have a heart attack just like your mom did at sixty, but you're currently forty-four. These are all examples of things you can get worked up about but have little to no control over.

Want an antidote to this terrible feeling? Control something small, in this moment, now. Find something you can have success with in the next five minutes, right now, today. Ever known someone who gets anxious before a big assignment and they want to clean their kitchen before they do their homework? Well, that is anxiety management in motion. Feel overwhelmed by your schedule? Take one thing off it. Feeling anxious about your weight? Put the Twinkies in the trash and go for a walk. Worried about an upcoming trip? Make a list of the items you want to pack. You get the idea. *Small control can equal big relief.*

Which small controls can you use to decrease stress and anxiety? Here is a list of my favorites. (By the way, I suggest giving yourself a ten-minute time limit for these small controls to make sure you don't turn a small control solution into a procrastination problem.)

Chapter 1: Calm Your Nerves

TRY ONE OF THESE IDEAS:

- Clean the kitchen.
- Take out the trash.
- Make a to-do list, bonus points if you can knock an item off it.
- Call a friend and catch up.
- Organize something, especially your desk.
- Delete old emails or computer files.
- Brush the cat, play ball with the dog, or watch the hamster run on that crazy metal wheel.
- Clean out your car.
- Take a five-minute walk outside to get fresh air.
- Focus on your breathing.
- Meditate.
- Empty the dishwasher.
- Pray.
- Change the sheets.
- Garden.
- Walk barefoot in the grass.
- Stretch, dance, do yoga, or otherwise move your body.

TACTIC #7
WRITE IT OUT

IT IS AN interesting thing in my practice: some clients love to write, but others absolutely hate it. Regardless of your love or not of writing, it can be helpful to write down what is bothering you. It seems like the act of writing something down, especially if you write by hand rather than type your woes, is incredibly freeing and relaxing. The relief seems to come with letting out the concern rather than letting it stew inside you.

How do you most effectively get pen to paper and get those gnawing worries out in the open? Well, I suggest grabbing a sheet of paper, journal, sticky note, whatever works. The goal here isn't to be grammatically correct, to form proper paragraphs, or even to put this on something you want to save. Rather you grab that pen and any handy paper and start scribbling down everything that is currently under your skin. Get it all out, even the silly stuff, including the stuff that you know better than to fret about but find yourself fretting about anyway. *Write it out, let it out.*

Sometimes it can be helpful to write "to" a specific individual, but it is rarely helpful to send this unedited, free flow of info to that individual. Thus, if you find yourself addressing your concerns to a certain person, whether on the page or a medium such as an email, make sure you then put away the paper, don't hit "send" on the email. Rather, let it sit for a day or two, then revisit, edit, and decide if it is worth sending along.

I have some clients who enjoy the process of writing and destroying their evidence, so to speak. They carry some shame or guilt about their worries, and the act of writing them down increases the shame that they will be found out, discovered, uncovered. So they will choose to do things like writing everything down and then shred, rip, tear, or burn the paper (carefully, please, with the burning). This can increase that freeing sensation and put a ritualized feel to your expression. Get it out and let it go.

Whatever method that suits you, from a formal daily journaling process to a quick scribble on a sticky note, whether you keep your musings forever or for three minutes, whether you cherish or destroy your writings, the point is to write it out to let it out. Get free from the worry.

APPLY THIS: Nerves taking over right now? Get yourself something to write with and write on and spend the next five minutes just putting it all out there. No matter if you are scribbling on the back of a napkin, writing in a fancy journal, or typing on your favorite electronic device, the point here is to write for five minutes. No editing, no proofreading, no judgment. Just get it out. Once your five minutes are up, you can choose what to do next. Keep or destroy; it doesn't matter. What matters is that you gave yourself a few minutes of relief.

TACTIC #8
GIVE YOURSELF A TIME FRAME

Sometimes we are worried about real, scary, big-time things. It happens when we have something major going on or coming up, from that big speech at the next convention to dealing with a friend with cancer. Often in these situations, we desperately want something specific to happen but have little control over the outcome. These types of worries tend to be unavoidable, and they are some of the worst worries to have because something truly frightening is making its mark in your world.

So what is a person to do when real life is really scary? Well, since you know you *are* going to worry about this issue, it makes sense to structure when and how you worry about it. I know—*planned worrying* sounds weird, but in practice, it works well. Setting aside dedicated time to worry leaves you freer to function during the rest of the day.

Now there will certainly be breakthrough worries and concerns, especially if the issue is one of the life biggies like illness, job change, death, financial catastrophe, etc. However, if you can train yourself to note those breakthrough thoughts and systematically put them off to your dedicated time, then you have a great system for managing a high level of worry and anxiety about a specific hard issue.

APPLY THIS: I typically suggest you set aside a specific time each day to dig into the worry, giving yourself a time limit for the fretting. It is especially helpful to write down your worries at this time and to give yourself a few minutes in the end to see if there are any questions you need to get answered or any plans of action you need to implement.

Let's say you choose 7:00 p.m. as your designated worry time. Then, during the rest of your day, when thoughts and concerns arise regarding this issue, quickly jot down those thoughts, and tell yourself, "I have time to worry about this at seven tonight." Write them down and then set them aside. When 7:00 p.m. comes, pull out your notes from the day and purposefully make the concern come up in your mind and body. Set a timer and let yourself dig into these feelings for fifteen to thirty minutes. Then when the timer rings (and I do suggest using a timer or an alarm as it helps alert the mind it's time to conclude), take a minute to review if there are any action steps to take. Then get up and move on with your night. This technique is a terrific one to manage worries that might otherwise keep you up at night.

TACTIC #9

DAILY RITUALS REALLY MAKE A DIFFERENCE*
*THE FIRST GOING DEEPER TIP

MOST OF US have small activities we can count on to lift our spirits. What are the little things that make you feel good? And how often do you do them?

It is always interesting to hear my clients, friends, and family members talk about what makes them feel good, and then indicate that they rarely let themselves pursue those activities. Often, we purposely deprive ourselves of these activities in the name of getting one more hour of work done, or watching that episode of the silly TV show you have already seen, or wasting time some other way.

An important habit to get into is peaceful intention: to set up and complete little calming activities in a ritualized fashion. Maybe it is sitting in the morning for five minutes with a cup of tea. Maybe it's meditating first thing when you get up for ten minutes (or right before bed if you're like me and mornings aren't your thing). It could be straightening up your workspace or house, reading from that inspirational book, going to your hockey league, softball night, or yoga class, attending church—all these activities deserve a place in your schedule, *sometimes even more than obligations you wouldn't dream of eliminating.*

If you can ritualize your self-care activities (another name for these small pleasures), they will be that much more effective. Rather than trying to squeeze them in last minute, in between obligations at home and work, you schedule them in *first* and then fit the obligations around them. Now, can you always do this? Probably not, but it is a great habit to get into, and once established, it tends to be no big deal to implement.

APPLY THIS: So please schedule your four days of exercise, taking your vitamins with your coffee in the morning or sitting in meditation every night at 9:30 p.m. before you go to bed. Give up that TV time to make room for inspirational reading each night. Block out time in your work schedule each day to take a ten-minute break outside; you know, that place where you can see the sun.

What would you like to add in? And when? I suggest making a list of your top best practices for self-care. I write them on a brightly colored sticky note and put it on my computer so I can check in with myself to make sure I got to most things on the list. A few of the things on my list right now are getting eight or more hours of sleep a night, drinking hot water with lemon (I know, it's weird, but it makes me feel good), checking in with my finances every Sunday night, and working out four or more days a week. What might be great little things on your best practices list?

Peek at your schedule and identify the small little behaviors (and maybe some bigger ones too) that make a difference to your mood, help calm you, and decrease your anxiety. Then *schedule your life around them, instead of the other way around.*

DAILY RITUALS WORKSHEET

Okay, let's identify your list here. Then grab a sticky note and write down the top five you want to focus on for the week.

Here are some ideas to get you started:

First, the three building blocks of health: Sleep, nutrition, and exercise.

_____

_____

_____

_____

Next, little treats for yourself. Put down things like smelling the flowers when you go to the grocery store, smiling more, being outside. You know, the little stuff that's free and lifts your mood.

_____

_____

_____

_____

Finally, the stuff you know is good for you, but you put off unless you schedule it in for sure, like meditation, or dealing with money, or calling your grandma—who lives three time zones away—before her bedtime.

_____

_____

_____

_____

Now pick your top five for the week, paste it on your computer or bathroom mirror, and go for it.

Chapter 1: Calm Your Nerves

TACTIC #10
TIME TO GIVE UP THE STIMULANTS*
*A GOING DEEPER TIP

THIS TIP IS probably the most unpopular suggestion I make to people. Seriously, when I tell folks that the single most effective way to decrease anxiety is to decrease caffeine, typically they look at me like I have three heads, and then they ask what they can do instead. I have received, ahem, "feedback" that asking someone to give up caffeine is a little like asking them to give up their right arm or first-born child or some other demand to that level of sacrifice.

Here is the bummer: Giving up caffeine *truly helps* decrease anxiety. And just in case you are feeling like shooting the messenger here, I am going to step out on a limb and make it worse by suggesting that, for some, switching to decaf isn't quite enough. You must give up the whole enterprise. Which, of course, means no coffee, no soda, no Monster energy drinks, and even limiting things like chocolate (and yes, I have put a security system around my house after writing this tip).

Curious what results I have seen from folks bravely taking on this suggestion? Well, I would venture to say, with some level of embarrassment frankly (I didn't need ten years of college to dispense this advice), that this is the *single best*, quickest to implement, most effective anxiety management technique I've got in my toolbox. I know—amazing, right? Give up caffeine and, unless you have attention deficit problems (caffeine acts opposite for these folks), you should notice an almost immediate decrease in symptoms of anxiety, especially decreasing your heart rate, sweating, and the "wired" feeling that you experience internally. Of course, for the truly anxious, then you have more work to do to get a handle on your anxious thoughts and behaviors, but a lack of caffeine is a huge head start in managing the worry.

APPLY THIS OVER THE NEXT WEEK OR SEVERAL WEEKS: If you are a major caffeine fiend, you will want to start small and gradually to prevent unpleasant withdrawal side effects like massive grouchiness and headaches. Try replacing one cup a day of caffeine with water for three days, and then add in a second replacement water, and so on. Maybe switch to half caffeine, half-decaf over a week or so, and then to decaf only, and so on. Trade the high-test coffee for green tea. Take your afternoon soda and replace it with a brisk walk. Consider shrinking the size of your caffeinated beverage. You know the drill: Cut it down and then test out what life is like without it. I bet you will notice an appreciable decrease in anxiety.

CHAPTER 2:
BEAT THE BLUES

TACTIC #11
THINK ABOUT YOUR THINKING

Here's another building block for you: Thought management. Humans have a special ability to think about our thinking. Now not too many other species have this trait, and none have it as well developed as we do. Think about it: When have you seen your dog think about how it thinks? Not so much, right?

Fido can remember that he gets in trouble when he jumps up and can learn not to jump up. Fluffy can learn (or not, as is the case with our most recent kitten) that using her claws when playing in the house gets her put outside, and she can then pattern herself to retract her claws when playing inside. Neither, however, can think to themselves, "Hmmm, Mom gets mad when I jump, Dad gets upset when I scratch him, maybe I need to think about a different strategy."

You, on the other hand, can think about your behavior, think about your feelings, and *think about your thinking*. This thinking about thinking is called metacognition.

What's cool about metacognition? Metacognition means we can think our way into a different way of thinking.

Let's look at the thoughts that most commonly run through your mind. Are you the type who is mostly content with what you have and where you are in life? If so, I bet your thoughts focus on that contentment, and occasionally you think about what's next. On the other hand, are you the type to be constantly thinking how awful, fat, lazy, or stupid (insert your favorite derogatory thought here) you are? Well, I bet your thoughts are primarily focused on that negative sense of yourself and your life since our thoughts build traction when we dwell on them.

APPLY THIS: When we stop ourselves by noticing the pattern of our thoughts (metacognition) and gradually, firmly, and repetitively bring ourselves back to a different thought pattern, we create new brain pathways that will help us be more in charge of our thinking. We can identify helpful and unhelpful patterns of thinking and determine what we want to keep giving time and attention to and which thoughts we just notice and then move on from. We can notice with amusement that the same silly thoughts keep trying to get traction, and instead of fretting about them, imagine letting them pass through.

TACTIC #12
SMILE MORE

YEARS AGO, I read a psychological study that took a group of folks diagnosed with depression and divided them into several groups. Now I can't remember the specifics of the study, name of the authors, or even the exact details of the setup, so bear with me, but it went something like this: The study participants were divided into three groups, with one group getting some sort of mental health treatment, one group who received no treatment at all, and one group was told to smile numerous times per day. Who got better the fastest? The smilers.

Why on earth would the smilers get better the fastest? According to scientists, there is some thought that facial feedback (first written about by Charles Darwin in 1872) can create emotion.[2] This is referred to as the "facial feedback hypothesis," which posits that facial movements (like smiling or frowning) drive emotional experience. So, frowning will increase negative feelings, smiling positive ones.

From a less scientific, more human standpoint, smiling connects us to others. Ever been having a bad day, and someone genuinely smiles at you, and suddenly you feel better? This works both ways, unfortunately, and speaks to why it is important to try to hang out with people who are making some attempt to emphasize life's upsides. Ever been having a good day, and someone comes home all grouchy? Next thing you know, your mood has deflated like a balloon, and you aren't smiling anymore. Conversely, you can help create a better mood for someone by having an encounter where you are warm and friendly, make eye contact, and smile. Literally, you can make someone's day doing this.

Maybe this smiling phenomenon is related to that concept we discussed in the last tip, where smiling more creates a new thinking pattern, which is linked to feeling happy, and then, because you are doing it more, you are feeling better. I don't know for sure. But what I do know is that life feels better for me when I'm smiling more, and I would guess it feels better for you too. Give it a try and make the time and effort to smile more throughout your day, and see if it makes a difference in how you feel.

APPLY THIS: Challenge yourself to smile at least five times daily for no reason at all. Then increase the challenge and smile, on purpose, at someone you would normally be neutral with, maybe your co-worker, the person passing you in the hall at school, or a check-out clerk. Don't just use this trick on strangers. Try smiling on purpose, genuinely, and with some frequency at your loved ones. Make eye contact and greet them with a big smile. You can even use this trick on yourself by smiling at your own sweet face in a mirror.

TACTIC #13
GET PHYSICAL

Be honest with me: when was the last time that you truly regretted going to the gym, or for a walk, or playing hoops, or hitting up that yoga class? (Don't get me started on regretting taking a run because I'm not a runner, and I always joke that I only run if someone is chasing me, and even then, I might just stop and try to talk them out of whatever their beef is.) Anyhoo, what I am trying to prod you into admitting is that even though you might often resist starting exercise, most of the time, you feel better afterward. Even if it was a sucky workout.

There are myriad studies that show even a minor amount of movement makes a difference in decreasing symptoms of sadness and anxiety, improving energy, and easing tension. Even couch potatoes don't have much of an excuse here since a measly ten minutes of not-very-brisk walking or riding a stationary bike at low intensity can make a difference. (This probably goes for other forms of exercise too; walking and biking was just the research I was checking out.)

I've seen several different studies suggesting that twenty minutes three to four times per week is a bit of a magic number, so this is a great goal to aim for. If that feels like too much, try starting with just a five-minute walk each day. Maybe you could add in a stroll with a loved one after dinner. Already a person who works out regularly? Maybe you add in different activities, try your workout outside, or have a friend join you for your typical routine.

The goal here isn't to become a triathlete (although that can be great too if it's your thing), but just to get your physical body moving. Physical movement boosts your neurotransmitters, the happy brain chemicals that enhance your mood. Your happy brain chemicals like movement, even if you have different parts of your brain trying to tell you otherwise. Ignore those thoughts that exercise is too hard, or too boring, or too time-consuming, or too taxing on your small reserve of energy, and just get going. All those thoughts that *prevent* you from getting in motion are the very thoughts that keep you stuck, emotionally and mentally, so you just can't let them have the final say.

Please check with your physician first if you have health concerns, of course, but almost everyone can benefit from some sort of movement, so get information on what type of movement will work the best for you.

START WORKING ON THIS: It can be tricky to convince your body and mind, especially if your mind is depressed and your body is "at rest," to get up and move, but this may be just the thing you need. Schedule it in, and don't worry about intensity as you are getting the routine established. Just get started and get in the habit of moving, and then improve from there. Don't be afraid to start small. Maybe you start by putting down this book and taking a walk around your building right now. Start with five minutes per day and build from there. Time to get moving.

TACTIC #14
SEEK SUPPORT

I WAS MEETING WITH a client the other day who was feeling down. She was complaining that she felt isolated from her friends but was also having trouble reaching out. Plus, she recognized that she was making the problem worse by not being available when her friends did call because she worried that she was a drag to hang out with. Not an inspiring cycle.

Loneliness and the blues indeed go together. It's a bit of a chicken and the egg issue since being blue decreases social interaction, and decreased social interaction can cause the blues. When you are feeling down, it can be hard to motivate yourself to be around others. It is also true that being down makes you think you *shouldn't* be around others. Then there is the little problem where being down *can* make it harder for others to want to hang around you.

Regardless of what came first (the social isolation or the blues), increasing social interaction can eliminate both problems. It is important, however, to choose *the right kind of social interaction to help yourself feel better.* Just getting together with a group and complaining about your problems can make you worse. Studies show, especially for girls and young women, that "co-ruminating" tends to make things worse because there is a tendency to talk too much about problems, thus dwelling on negative emotions and experiences. Then you are stuck in the negativity cycle, making it harder and harder to manage emotions.

APPLY ONE OF THESE IDEAS: So, what are you supposed to do? Well, it can be important to vent and be heard, but it is almost as important to then seek solutions and to try different approaches. Options for support can be more formal, like therapy or a support group, or less formal, like a friend or group of friends you can talk to. Organized support can sometimes be found in communities like a church or temple, neighborhood gatherings, or monthly organized meetings such as a hiking club, book club, mom's co-op, or other group social activities. It is less important what the get-together is about and more important to go and build some connections.

If you struggle with social skills or are truly depressed, it can be helpful to go to a group therapy meeting facilitated by a professional therapist. If you typically have reasonable social skills but are adjusting to a new life situation such as a divorce, single parenting, move, or job change, check out something in your community. One easy way to break into a new social group is to do something relating to an interest you already have.

Try a variety of things until you find the fit that helps you feel a little more connected, less lonely, and more involved. It can be as simple as picking up the phone and making a quick connection with a friend or as involved as joining a new group activity. Whatever your choice, reach out and practice being around others.

TACTIC #15
MOVE AWAY FROM THOSE SUBSTANCES

How many of you know someone who reaches for the bottle, the pack of cigarettes, or even something a little stronger when he or she feels down? Do you do it yourself? Maybe you rationalize it by saying, "I had a hard day; I need a beer." Maybe you are like an incredible growing number of people in Colorado who are using marijuana daily to manage their moods (for those of you who aren't in Colorado, we have legalized marijuana). Maybe you know someone who had a quick outpatient surgery but has never quite got off the painkillers that were only supposed to last a few weeks. Drinking wine every night? How many glasses? Still chewing tobacco even though you meant to quit on your birthday?

All of these are substances that impact our moods. Now most of them, in the moment, help you feel a little more relaxed, a little less tense and take the edge off. The problem is that reaching for substances to manage your mood, particularly when you abuse them (use too much or use them too often) is that you are stressing your neurotransmitters (the marvelous chemicals in your brain that manage your mood), making it more difficult in the long run for your body's natural processes to manage your mood. You are risking addiction, which is a whole nasty issue in and of itself; you *really* don't want to add to the list of things you need to fix in your life. Finally, you are just putting off the inevitable. Feeling crummy? Well, when you use substances, it only puts off that crummy feeling and often compounds it later.

APPLY IT: While it sounds tough, it is a great idea to reach for those crutches a little less often and in limited quantities. For some of us, moderation isn't enough, and we need to "just say no," to everything, especially if we are feeling extremely down and certainly if addiction is a problem. It is important not to fool yourself into thinking that drinking or using is truly helping you solve your problems. Start by recognizing that the substance is a temporary source of relaxation, calming energy, or whatever "lift" you use it for. Then question if this is something that you truly need (in which case you may need to look at the possibility you are addicted and should get some help). Challenge yourself to use healthier means to manage your mood rather than checking out.

Start by taking a good hard look at your use patterns, and then see if you can reach for something healthy instead. Maybe a walk instead of wine? A car ride instead of a cigarette? Gardening instead of reaching for the weed? Try to cut down a little, and then think about challenging yourself to cut down a lot. Start small and go from there.

TACTIC #16
THOUGHTS, FEELINGS, AND BEHAVIORS

OPERATING BEHIND THE scenes in our lives is a constant interaction between our thoughts, behaviors, and feelings. All three are like finely tuned instruments, where any change in one of the elements affects the other two. The bad news? This means that things we think, do, or feel affect how we think, behave, and feel. The good news? How we think, what we do, and how we feel affect how we think, behave, and feel.

So how do you shift your thoughts, feelings, or behaviors? How much impact can a person *really* have over these things? According to happiness researchers and positive psychologists, we are born with a certain disposition that makes up about 50 percent of our happiness equation. Only about 10 percent of our happiness can be accounted for by external events, even the big ones.[3] (This helps explain why lottery winners who fully expect they will be incredibly happy forever due to their winnings revert to their pre-win levels of happiness, typically within a year or so after winning.)

The truly excellent news is that the remaining 40 percent of our individual happiness equation is up to us. With a full 40 percent at your disposal, how are you creating happiness for yourself? Are you taking charge of your thoughts, feelings, and behaviors to make a lasting, positive impact in your life? Not quite sure how to undo that complicated relationship between thoughts, feelings, and behaviors?

APPLY ONE OF THESE HELPFUL IDEAS:

The most effective pattern is to shift actions first, then thoughts tend to come around a bit; finally, feelings will shift. Take the time and care to implement a variety of positive, healthy, active behaviors to help you manage your mood (there are about one hundred suggestions in this book alone). When you notice something is getting you down, take care to think clearly about the situation, relax into a feeling of goodness, and take positive action to solve the problem. Thinking strategically looks like accepting things as they are and then moving toward productive action instead of beating yourself up. For example: "I may not know how to address this situation yet, but if I relax a little, over time, I will discover new ideas and creative solutions."

Cut the string between negative thoughts, feelings, and behaviors by deliberately interrupting the typical chain of events. (For example, you stub your toe when you get out of bed, think to yourself, *I'm going to have a lousy day*, and then yell at other drivers on your way into work.) Instead, try to shorten the duration of the problem and move forward to acceptance as quickly as you can. (You stub your toe when you get out of bed, think to yourself, *That hurt. Oh well, moving on.* And reorient into setting yourself up for success in your day.)

TACTIC #17
BALANCING STRENGTHS AND WEAKNESSES

My practice specializes in treating anxiety and trauma. This means that I hear about a tremendous amount of pain in people's lives. There are stories of traumatic events, accidents, cruelty by others (these are always the worst for people), and huge, crushing life disappointments. What is striking, though, is that when people start to feel better, they almost always take a perspective that they are stronger or more resilient or *better* somehow because they made it through whatever terrible experience brought them into therapy. They have struck a balance of finding strengths within bad experiences.

We too have an opportunity to balance out our strengths and weaknesses. All of us have a series of strengths and weaknesses in our personalities, attributes, and overall life experiences. Most of these strengths and weaknesses, since they are lifelong traits of personality, or caused by childhood experiences, aren't going anywhere anytime soon. This is great news because we know what we have to work with. We can admit that most aspects of our personality aren't a big surprise at this point.

Now those of you out there who are starting to lament that you only have weaknesses and have never been good at anything, hang on. All of us have a combination of both strengths and weaknesses, and, for most of us, many of these traits are simply two sides of the same coin.

Stubborn? Okay, this may make you hardheaded at times, but I would also bet you get taken advantage of less often. Super sensitive? Well, this may feel annoying when you cry at the drop of a hat, but I would also guess this same sensitivity makes you more approachable than others and extra empathetic when someone is telling you about their issues.

For every negative thought, situation, person, or experience you are currently feeling down about, try to challenge yourself to see the other side of the coin. Try to identify one upside that your "issue" is bringing to you in addition to the pain. Sometimes you need to make up an imagined future positive scenario to make things feel better. This is even possible when it feels like there is no flip side. For example, a dear friend had to put his parents in assisted living a while back. It felt defeating to the parents and horrible to my friend who wished he could house his parents. The flipside? Knowing that they were safe and that their basic needs were being taken care of in a way no one working adult could provide.

APPLY THIS: When you are feeling down, take a few minutes and challenge yourself to identify possible positives that can come out of this hard situation/relationship/day/whatever. See if you can see the flip side of the equation and/or notice sweet options that could possibly come up out of this stuff that feels like a drag. Write them down, talk about them, make your realization public if you can, so it will stick in your mind. Acceptance is all about looking at both sides of a situation instead of getting mired in rigid, negative thinking that keeps us stuck.

TACTIC #18
BOUNCE BACK

IN MY PRACTICE, I am always looking at the differences, large and small, between the folks who get better and the folks who don't do so well. A major difference I keep seeing over and over relates to our increasingly famous friend, *resiliency*. Folks who possess factors of resiliency have the tools and attitude to bounce back from adversity and move forward with their lives. Folks who use less of these factors tend to stay stuck, feel helpless and powerless, and set themselves up for failure instead of success.

A twenty-year study on resiliency by Dr. Salvatore R. Maddi found three predictive factors supporting what I see in my practice.[4] The predictive factors are attitudes that lead to behaviors that help a person take adversity and turn it into an advantage. First, there is commitment, then control, and finally, challenge.

Commitment means you are taking the bull by the horns. You commit to be involved, push yourself to be out in the world. This is like my client who felt he was losing everything (house, girlfriend, job) at the same time. Instead of giving up and isolating, he pushed himself to take up running and train for an upcoming race. It was one thing he knew he could commit to following through on since all this other stuff was outside his direct ability to change.

Then there is control. Control is all about taking something that feels beyond your control and trying to make as much of it as possible in your control. Now you don't just have the bull by the horns; you are showing it where to go. Trying to influence the outcome of your adversity and push through the trouble gives you a sense of power and keeps powerlessness from taking over. The same client who was in the middle of losing everything took control over his housing search and his job search, giving himself weekly goals to meet (three applications sent out per week, that sort of thing).

Finally, there is an attitude of challenge. My friend and genius businessman Chuck Blakeman describes "opportunities cleverly disguised as problems" as a life philosophy.[5] He spends so much less time worried than most people I know because he is steadfast in his belief that pretty much every problem houses a secret opportunity. Everything is simply a challenge to manage, an opportunity to learn from, not a problem to be overwhelmed by.

APPLY THIS: The next time you feel oppressed by a problem, take a moment to commit to solving it, see it as a challenge to tackle, and attempt to control the outcomes within your reach. Be like my client, who took huge adversity and stubbornly set his mind toward coming out on top by having a can-do attitude, landing on his feet. Push yourself instead of giving in to passivity. And remember, any movement in this direction, no matter how small, will start to build your resilience.

TACTIC #19
INVEST IN A SPIRITUAL PRACTICE
*A GOING DEEPER TIP

The topics of spirituality and religion can be divisive ones, so I will attempt to tread carefully here, but it is worth examining, not the least because research clearly suggests that well-being and spiritual practice go hand-in-hand.

Contrary to popular belief, spirituality isn't necessarily about going to church. There are multiple definitions of spirituality, and all are based on a relationship between people and something bigger than themselves. Some common ways to access spirituality are:

- Exploring connection with nature
- Understanding and savoring your heritage, ancestry, or culture
- Connecting with things larger than yourself such as God, the universe, or spirit

Spirituality is certainly a personal experience and can range from brief connections when outside in nature ("I suddenly feel more open and free") to a much more structured, formal, religious practice. The notion of positive spirituality suggests constructs like building and enhancing relationships with ourselves, others, and the world around us, increasing global understanding and connection, focusing on love and hope, and connecting to things greater than ourselves.

The best spiritual experiences build belonging, increase our sense of liberation, and make us sensitive to the sacred. They help make us aware of what is truly precious. We should take great care to avoid practices, sometimes mislabeled as spiritual or religious, which build narratives of hatred, separation, and superiority, as these constructs increase distance between ourselves and others, build a platform of fear, and can lead to violence and oppression.

Having a positive spiritual connection can help you beat the blues in many ways, including increasing connection with others, helping you see larger connections in the world, and decreasing the feeling it's just you out there by yourself, combating a hostile world.

APPLY THIS: One of my favorite suggestions for clients with a spiritual or religious practice is to separate what is their work as an individual from those things that are beyond control and can be handed over to the universe, God, goddess, divine wisdom (please use whatever word or description makes the most sense to you). Now you can stress less, handing over what is beyond you, so you can focus on what you *can* handle, what *is* in your control, and what *is* your work. Confronting a situation that seems larger than what you can handle? Hand it over, send it upstairs, ask for some universal support. Then go about what you *can* manage.

TACTIC #20
WHEN THE BLUES ARE SOMETHING MORE SERIOUS
*A GOING DEEPER TIP

Contrary to popular belief, real clinical depression is significantly different from and more serious than a bout of sadness or even an experience of grief. Depression is an illness, not a character flaw, and it is one of the most common, treatable forms of mental illness.

People with depression experience significant changes in their interest in and ability to take pleasure from their daily activities. They tend to struggle with eating, causing either weight gain or loss. They struggle with insomnia, have trouble falling asleep, and often wake much earlier than they would prefer. Sometimes they will oversleep and even have trouble getting out of bed at all. They will demonstrate a lack of energy others can notice just by looking at them. Difficulty with concentration is common, as is trouble with memory. Feelings of worthlessness, hopelessness, and guilt are a frequent part of the depressive experience. Recurrent thoughts of death or suicide can occur.

Sadness is a more transitory experience and tends to have an easily identifiable trigger. Sadness is something that you can feel along with other emotions; for example, you feel sad about something not working out, but you can also think with some excitement about something enjoyable coming up. Someone with depression, on the other hand, will feel down, sad, and generally terrible and have an extremely difficult time feeling anything but these challenging feelings. Even when the good stuff is right in front of them, jumping up and down.

Grief, another form of the blues, is caused by a loss of a loved one, pet, job, important dream, or other life experience. Grief includes sadness as one element of a complex experience and tends to have distinct stages a person progresses through over time (See Elisabeth Kubler-Ross's old school but still excellent book *On Death and Dying* for more info).[6] Therefore, it is possible to be grieving and not depressed, and it can also be possible for depression and grief to occur at the same time.

If you suspect you may have depression, don't struggle with it by yourself. It is not a matter of willpower, toughness, strength, or weakness. Despite what well-meaning friends or relatives might tell you, you can't "pull up your bootstraps" and beat depression. Depression is a true illness, and there are a variety of effective treatments available, including therapy, medication, and other evidence-based approaches. Unfortunately, despite depression being so common, typically less than a third of the sufferers ever seek treatment, and these numbers drop to precipitously low levels if you are of racial minority descent.

Depression makes your brain trick you into believing that life is not worth living, that others aren't on your side, and that you are hopeless and helpless. Don't believe these lies; get the help you need so you can get back to enjoying life, even with its ups and downs.

CHAPTER 3:
KNOCK OUT ANGER

TACTIC #21
FIRST, SEEK TO UNDERSTAND: WHAT MAKES ME MAD?

Despite the bad rap it gets, anger is a crucial member of our emotional family. It serves an especially important purpose, which is to alert us when our boundaries are threatened. Anger lets us know something about what is important to us. Anger can range from low-level emotions like annoyance or irritation to the big daddy of the emotional spectrum, a full-blown rage. And anger is complicated because it sometimes isn't just about being pissed off. Often, anger is covering up other (even less fun) emotions like hurt, fear, or the feelings incurred by injustice.

Anger becomes problematic in three main ways:

First, it is the emotion that most easily disconnects us from logic and can lead to explosive, impulsive reactions that do not represent our long-term interests. (Think exploding on the airline employee and getting kicked off your flight.) Folks who feel and express anger in this manner can be referred to as having explosive anger.

Second, it can be turned inward, suppressed, and held onto, creating burning resentments and causing stress on your emotional and physical systems. (Think hating your boss and feeling worse and worse about coming into work until you make yourself sick.) These folks have what is called implosive anger.

Third, regardless of whether you experience anger in an explosive or implosive manner, anger and happiness do not cohabitate well. Feeling mad crowds out positive feelings and experiences, impedes communication, upsets relationships, and is hard for your body to process. Anger increases the output of stress hormones and has even been linked to cardiovascular problems.

Interested in dealing with anger more elegantly? Start by understanding your typical anger pattern. Categorize your anger experience: Are you an exploder or an imploder? How frequently are you pissed off, and why? List your top triggers and your typical responses. Notice your riskiest times and situations for anger. Maybe you are the type of person (like me) who melts down if they are extremely hungry. Maybe you are like one of my best friends who gets incredibly irritable if she goes three days without exercise. Maybe you are like my client who is a human thunderstorm on the road. Like being in charge? I bet you get mad when things aren't going your way.

APPLY THIS: First, seek to understand your anger. Know your triggers and try to work around them *before* you are mad. If you tend to be the exploding kind, your work will be to better manage your outward expression of anger: taking breaks and thinking before responding when angry. If you tend to internalize your anger or, even worse, pretend you're never mad, you will likely need to work on admitting and expressing your feelings rather than stuffing them. In all cases, understanding how you get mad and catching yourself before you are furious will go a long way to managing your anger. You are human; hence, you will sometimes be angry. You can plan for it.

TACTIC #22
HOW TO RELAX WHEN YOU'RE ABOUT TO EXPLODE

You know it would be better to cool off. Once you're calm, you're in a much better place to deal with an anger situation, no matter the source. People tell you, "It's easy. Just count to ten before you do anything." Or they'll tell you to take some deep breaths. Maybe they say to count to ten backward. Or whatever. So why aren't these incredibly "easy" situations working for you?

Well, one problem is that anger tends to come up so fast there doesn't seem to be time to fend it off. Anger affects your mind and body quickly because it is governed by a small part of your brain called the amygdala that senses when you are under threat and triggers a slew of chemicals to release into your bloodstream so you can act fast with lots of energy. These changes occur with little involvement of the part of your thinking brain that weighs pros and cons and comes up with reasonable decisions. This arrangement is by design—our caveman ancestors couldn't stop to weigh options when they got cornered by a tiger. This is why instincts exist. But chances are good you aren't confronting actual tigers, so you need a different strategy. The key here is to try to notice when you feel threatened and then train your body and mind how to think through the threat rather than lash out against it.

Using a combination of responses is your best bet to get your thinking brain back on track and be more in charge of your emotional and instinctual responses. You will want to implement a few different strategies to give your brain the space to figure out your options and respond rather than react.

TRY THIS: First, take a deep breath. Next, press your hands together, *hard*, for a count of ten. (Most people go way too fast if they just count because of their extra energy, so use the good ole' "one Mississippi, two Mississippi" method.) Then stop pressing but keep your palms and fingers together and take two deep breaths. Tell yourself you can relax, calm down, and think. Next, stretch your arms and hands out in front of you and take a breath. Now give yourself a hug, squeezing your upper arms and shoulders, and count to ten. Whatever arm was on top, switch so the other side is on top, and hug again for a count of ten. Take more deep breaths. Notice the sensations in your body, and imagine the anger and tension are draining out of your body. Tell yourself, again, that you can calm down, relax, and think. Repeat until you can think clearly about your anger and what you would like to do about whatever situation is so unpleasant. Or scary. Or threatening. Even though it's probably not an actual tiger.

Don't worry about anyone seeing you doing this. This technique can be done quietly, almost anywhere, and if others notice at all, they'll probably think you are stretching (which, of course, you are, among other things). Resist the urge to snap "What are you looking at?" and instead calm down that threat response until you can think through your options.

TACTIC #23

WHAT DO HUNGER, LONELINESS, FEELING TIRED, OR BEING STRESSED HAVE TO DO WITH ANGER? THE HALTS PRINCIPLE

While growing up, I remember my lovely mom telling my brother and me to "HALT: Never get too hungry, angry, lonely, or tired." She was trying to help us manage our moods and understand where stuff was coming from when we felt down. As an adult, in my therapy work, I have long used the HALT principle with my clients. Here's the thing: a large portion of the problems people seek care for boil down to not taking good care of themselves. They often forget to eat, are stuffing anger, not sleeping, not connecting with others, and/or feeling extremely stressed out. Watch out for the HALTS: never get too hungry, angry, lonely, tired, or stressed.

While watching out for the HALTS is a good start, there is something important about the anger portion of the principle. Anger can be caused by the HLT and S of the formula. Ever heard about someone being "hangry"? It means they are so hungry that they are angry. When folks are lonely and feel disconnected, it is easy to get angry and resentful of others, especially those who seem to have everything all together and have lots of friends. Feeling tired? Well, that is a recipe for getting irritable. When was the last time you were sleep-deprived and felt cheerful? Never, right? Then there is the overarching issue of stress. Stress takes up a tremendous amount of mental energy, is corrosive to our physical bodies, and can lead to short tempers, increased irritability, and tense interpersonal exchanges.

APPLY THIS: The next time you find yourself feeling cranky, take a peek at the HALTS principle. How are you doing on your self-care basics? Are you feeding yourself well? How is your sleep? Are you feeling connected to others or struggling with loneliness? How much stress are you under?

Take some time to get something to eat, make a meal plan for the next few days, go to that awesome place called the grocery store, then make yourself something yummy to eat. Let yourself take a nap, make yourself turn off the TV or video games, and go to bed before midnight. Rest. Spend a weekend not doing anything. Sleep in. I know it sounds incredible, but I assure you that people do these things.

Lost your mojo for social stuff? Challenge yourself to reach out to a long-lost friend. Make small connections with people throughout your day. Plan a girls' trip or a guys' night out. Tell your neighbor his hydrangeas are a thing of awesome and spectacular beauty.

Manage your stress by setting up a healthy schedule for yourself. Exercise consistently: Brief walks around the block and plank pose while your chai is heating up all count. Take care of your body and your brain by managing existing stress and decreasing stress over time.

Apply the HALTS principle, and you might be amazed by how much better you feel. Not to mention the incredible freedom of taking good care of yourself.

TACTIC #24
MAY THE COOL THOUGHTS WIN

Ever seen a mob before? Hopefully, you were safely in your living room, watching the news and shaking your head about some crazy fan base showing their support (or opposition) of a team by rioting. Whether watching at a distance or being smack in the middle of one of those experiences, what's important is to notice how people inflame the situation. People will throw words, signs, slogans, and objects to make others get riled up, angry, and reactive. If someone tries to talk sense into the crowd, the mob will often up the ante, creating more chaos by getting individual people worked up into a collective frenzy.

Anger works a little like a riot in our brains. Once we get riled up, we tend to be on the lookout for evidence that we are right, this situation is terrible, and we deserve to feel awful. We inflame ourselves with thoughts like *This always happens; he is never on time; my boss is such a jerk* (or insert your preferred curse word or insult here—my current favorite is *jack wagon*); *she is the worst nag; my life is ruined.* All these thoughts fall into the "hot thought" category. This is your mind collaborating with your anger in a way that is almost guaranteed to make you feel worse. It cuts off solutions and focuses you on a huge problem, even if the problem is only a small- or medium-sized one. Notice how these hot thoughts make the issue in question large and solid—there's nothing like the words "always" and "never" to rile us up and rile us up quick. There is little flexibility or understanding but a lot of negative labeling.

Cool thoughts, on the other hand, are the types of thoughts that increase flexibility, help you think about many options, give yourself and others more latitude, increase understanding, and make things temporary instead of permanent. These types of thoughts examine a person's in-the-moment behavior instead of characterizing the behavior as a long-term personality flaw. (It is so much harder to change a fixed personality trait than a momentary mistake.)

Cool thoughts sound like, *Boy, it is frustrating that this has happened more than once, I will have to speak to him about being on time, Maybe my boss is having a bad day, She might be as frustrated as I am, I am having a hard fifteen minutes*, or, even the general acceptance of reality expressed by *Wow, life sucks this month*. Cool thoughts move you toward solutions by helping you think through multiple options. Cool thoughts calm you down and let you move away from a problem by making it temporary, shrinking the issue, giving yourself permission to feel the feeling but not get lost in it. Cool thoughts are rational, logical, sensible, reasoned. You know, cool.

USE THIS TO COOL DOWN: Replacing hot thoughts with cool thoughts is almost always helpful. Ask yourself to make this an "in the moment" issue; resist the urge to globalize. Change your language from "always" and "never" to "right now" and "today." See if you can focus on one piece of evidence instead of bringing up every perceived slight in the last several years. Ask for what you want instead of raging at the other person. You get the idea. Cool down first. Then respond.

TACTIC #25
DON'T HIT ANYTHING, EXCEPT MAYBE THE PAVEMENT

A WHILE BACK, THERE was a popular psychology movement to vent your anger by acting aggressively toward inanimate objects. This led to folks beating up their pillows and mattresses, smashing glass bottles against walls, shooting at trees in the woods, driving too fast, and generally thinking that they would calm down if they acted out. It seems logical, right? We feel bad, and so we need to get that "bad" out of our system.

Recent research suggests this is not so helpful. Acting out can increase blood pressure and adrenaline levels, both of which are counter to the things your body needs to calm down. This type of elevation creates more tension instead of releasing it, which is our goal, especially for an explosive anger experiencer. In addition, these types of outbursts, even when deliberate, create a negative reaction model in your brain, making it subsequently more difficult to calm down the next time you are angry. Plus, it's not always going to be a good time to shoot at trees.

DO THIS INSTEAD: Instead of acting out your anger, especially through aggressive behaviors like hitting, slamming, throwing, etc., try going out for a more productive physical outlet. Run, jump, do some push-ups, race your own best time. Try tai chi, go to the playground with your child and swing on the monkey bars, play fetch with your dog or Frisbee with your friends. If you are attracted to the heavy bag at the gym or that kickboxing class, make sure it is a focused approach. Try to beat your last record, focus on form, count your reps. Whatever your physical activity, from an easy walk to a major workout, let those endorphins get you going in a positive and healthy direction.

For explosive types, even a workout may be too engaging at that moment, so wait a bit and start by calmly walking, and increase your intensity once you are less angry.

For implosive types, working out is a great way to acknowledge and release angry feelings before you stuff them down.

Overall, deliberate physical activity is a more productive use of your riled-up energy than aggressive actions, even if you have to calm down the intensity of the exercise. When you give yourself even just twenty minutes of activity, you feed your neurotransmitters good chemicals while channeling all that negative, aggressive energy. And no trees or pillows have to pay for what went wrong in your world.

TACTIC #26
MAKING MOLEHILLS OUT OF MOUNTAINS

Ever had a rip-roaring fight with a friend, and later neither of you can even remember what you were both so upset about? That's because a huge part of how anger manages to lead us into stupid behavior is by distorting how we see and size up the situation at hand. When we are boiling mad, we become convinced that our self-respect and well-being are dependent on how we react *this very second*. It feels like delay will be seen as a sign of vulnerability and weakness that will make friends, family, co-workers, and even total strangers mock us. This is how anger undermines the decision-making part of our brains and pushes us quickly down the road to bad reactions and dumb deeds.

Counteracting this tendency isn't easy. The first step is to breathe and let yourself get some distance from the anger abyss. Then it can be helpful to ask yourself and your anger a number of questions. Questions like, "Why am I so bloody pissed off right now? Is this a new or different problem? What is really going on here? Is all this anger going to help me solve this problem?"

Use your mental time machine to project yourself into the future. Think long-term. Now imagine you are five years in the future. Do you think you will even be able to remember this conflict? Most likely not, which makes this not such a big deal anymore, eh? If this *is* one of those giant catastrophes, maybe you *will* be able to remember it five years from now, but my guess is that you would prefer to look back on this great big thing and feel proud of your restraint and be glad that you didn't add an explosion to an already unpleasant event.

Remember that this is one moment in a long life. If it's a relationship problem, remember that this is one moment in the relationship, no more and no less. Your identity at work, your value as a friend, your dynamic with your spouse or lover—these are all founded on hundreds if not thousands of interactions and behaviors. There will be other opportunities for you to address the need posed by this moment.

You do not know for sure what you will be thinking and feeling about this tomorrow, or the next day, or next week, or next year. But you will almost certainly not be feeling about it as intensely as you are now.

APPLY THIS: Don't let anger get the best of you in this moment. Use your brain to calm your emotions by thinking about your future. Let yourself imagine all the positives just waiting for you out there. Imagine how silly and unimportant this experience will be five years from now. Then choose your reaction and move on. It is, indeed, terrible that he or she was late *again* or forgot to pick up that thing you said you needed, but you will live to fight another day and enjoy life more if you give yourself the chance to address these crimes in a calmer frame of mind.

TACTIC #27
RECALL YOUR VALUES
*A GOING DEEPER TIP

I OFTEN JOKE WITH my clients that I have a "very cheesy toolbox" and then gesture grandly to an imaginary box while describing said imaginary toolbox as purple and sparkly, with a huge array of marvelous tools, tips, and tricks inside. One of the many cheesy things I bring out of this very cheesy toolbox is the concept of being your best self. Your best self is the person your dog thinks you are. Your best self is made up of the best bits of you: knowing who you are, understanding what is important to you, behaving in ways that make you feel proud of yourself.

One of the problems with anger is that it takes us away from behaving like our best selves. When angry, we tend to be reactive and unkind, lapsing into yelling, swearing, or even violence. Later, we usually feel like a jerk, and that's putting it mildly. Sometimes we even incur terribly negative consequences like losing our job, losing a friend, or even losing our freedom. (Think: jail.)

Anger decreases our ability to perceive reality, and when our perceptions are off, we behave unreasonably. Once we are behaving unreasonably, it is hard to stop ourselves until it is too late, and we have done something we regret. This is why anger is sometimes referred to as "temporary insanity." We truly aren't cognizant of what we are saying, how we are saying it, what we're doing, or how other people are feeling about our behavior when we are in a rage. After the storm is over, then we have to face the consequences of our unreasonable reactions, and this is not pretty. When we act in a way from a place that is so vastly different from our best self, we feel lousy.

Chapter 3: Knock Out Anger

One of the best ways to prevent this type of problem from occurring is to think about your values. This works best if you remind yourself about your values *before* you are angry, but it can also be helpful in the moment. Setting an intention for how you want to behave, in accordance with your values, will help you function when tough emotions surface. And since many interactions are reasonably predictable, you can set yourself up by practicing this intention over time. For example, I bet that annoying co-worker pushes your buttons in similar ways throughout the week. Thus, on Sunday you can decide what your values are, and how your best self would respond. On Monday, and through the week, you can then practice responding more like your best self, holding your values in the front of your mind each time they inevitably annoy you by telling that obnoxious story about how they saved the day with a client for the millionth time.

Get the picture? Identify your values, choose what is truly important to you, and then plan to be that person in the middle of a conflict. Breathe and reconnect with that intention before you let someone else bear the brunt of your anger. If you slip, try to reconnect as soon as possible with your best self. You can even say something like, "I'm sorry. That didn't come out right; what I meant was _____." Know your values, intend to behave like your best self, and then keep practicing, moment by moment.

RECALL YOUR VALUES: VALUES LIST

Sample Values List: Here are ninety-nine common values I smashed together from personal experience and a bunch of lists I found online. Some will describe you perfectly; some won't be the right fit at all. Please take a peek and circle the ones that make the most sense to you, and scribble in any I have missed. Then pare down to your top ten, and finally, choose your top three that inform your life. My current top three are connection, joy, and adventure. What are yours?

Acceptance	Faith	Organization
Achievement	Family	Originality
Adventure	Flexibility	Passion
Ambition	Focus	Personal development
Appreciation	Freedom	Pleasure
Art/creativity	Friendship	Power
Assertiveness	Generosity	Prosperity
Authority	Growth	Reliability
Balance	Happiness	Resilience
Beauty	Harmony	Resolve
Belonging	Health	Reputation
Boldness	Helping	Respect
Calm	Honesty	Responsibility
Certainty	Honor	Risk-taking
Cheerfulness	Humility	Sacrifice
Community	Humor	Security
Compassion	Integrity	Self-control
Competence	Intelligence	Sensitivity
Confidence	Intuition	Significance
Connection	Joy	Spirituality
Cooperation	Justice	Spontaneity
Courage	Kindness	Stability
Country	Knowledge	Strength
Curiosity	Leadership	Status
Dependability	Learning	Success
Determination	Love	Teamwork
Discipline	Loyalty	Trust
Diversity	Making a difference	Understanding
Drive	Mindfulness	Uniqueness
Empathy	Motivation	Variety
Enthusiasm	Nature	Warmth
Excellence	Open-mindedness	Wisdom
Fairness	Optimism	Wonder

TACTIC #28
RELEASE THE RIGHTEOUSNESS

One of the things that fuels anger, like pouring gasoline on a fire, is the idea that you are right. Not just a little bit correct, mind you, but that tricky place where you think you are *right* and someone else is *wrong*. This place of righteousness tends to feed those hot thoughts of anger and keeps the flames going by feeding your brain thoughts like *I can't believe he did that; I would never say that; I've never been that way; She is always such an idiot; I can't believe this is happening to me again*. Righteous thoughts tend to put us in two categories, making us both the innocent victim of someone else's behavior and elevating our behavior over someone else's, often at the same time.

Ever been in a fight with your significant other and thought to yourself that you are 100 percent right and she/he is 100 percent wrong? How well does that conversation go when you deliver your assessment of the other person's total and complete wrongness? I imagine not so well. When you are super-duper sure of your rightness, strangely enough, they often come back thinking they are 100 percent right, and you are the person in the wrong. The fight quickly rockets past whatever the original trigger was and becomes about who is more wrong.

Remember that old expression about it "taking two to tango"? When you can take ownership of your part of the equation, things tend to go better for both people in the argument. Releasing this notion that you are somehow an innocent victim helps you understand what part you may have played in escalating a fight. If you can also stop thinking you are better than your opponent, you can see not only how you may have contributed to the conflict but how it feels to be on the receiving end. What if you disagree? That doesn't make you better or them worse; it just means you are not on the same page.

Understanding where someone else is coming from can make all the difference in resolving a problem with compassion and care versus with anger and frustration. Release that righteousness and take ownership of your own contributions. The problem will likely make lots more sense and be easier to solve than sticking to your perfect 100 percent guns that you are right and someone else is wrong, wrong, wrong.

 Ask yourself what your responsibility is in the situation upsetting you. Maybe you used a harsh tone when you asked for something, or you came at someone too aggressively. Or too passive-aggressively. Consider that you may need to soften your approach and ask instead of demand for your needs to be met. Try to use a percentage model (especially when you don't think you're in the wrong), like "I am responsible for 25 percent of this conflict, Sally is responsible for 50 percent, and our dumb work deadline probably made us both tense and deserves 25 percent of the blame." These approaches increase your understanding of what is behind the problem and give you more options for solutions. It is a rare, rare day when (if you are human) you own zero percent of a problem. Own up, and you can move forward more quickly.

TACTIC #29

WHEN ALL ELSE FAILS, WALK AWAY

I MUST ADMIT, I'M not looking forward to Thanksgiving dinner this election season because no matter who wins, it's going to be ugly. It's going to be one of those dinners where I am going to get cornered by my close-talker neighbor and hear all about political opinions that are the polar opposite of my own. Or like my own but expressed in an undignified way that makes me feel kind of dumb for sharing the same beliefs with this individual. This is the kind of stuff that gets under a person's skin. It feels so important, even vital, to share your opinion and make your point. It's impossible. How can you make your point when someone else wants to make theirs at your expense? Ugh—so annoying.

When you're angry or on the receiving end of someone else's anger, you want help *right now*. What is the thing that works the best? The quickest? What will calm you down the most? How do you manage when there is no winning solution in sight?

Two words: Walk away.

Don't try to say anything witty, don't press your point, and don't try to make the other person calm down. Just take a breath, let the other person know you aren't going to engage now, and take a break by physically removing yourself from the situation. Hang up the phone, walk into the next room, go sit in your car, take a walk around the building, go to the bathroom and lock yourself in a stall. Just take a break.

The main goal of anger management is to control the expression of your strong, angry emotions while simultaneously reducing the physiological effects of anger (red face, hands balled up into fists, tight chest). Your goal is to reduce the emotion, decrease the pumping adrenaline, and figure out a way to get your needs met without damaging anyone in the process. Paradoxically, sometimes the absolute best way to get closer to a good solution is to take a few minutes to disengage. *Break the mood* and get yourself back to your thinking, calm, reasonable self. Then you can deal.

For those of you who are close to someone who has a hard time when you disengage, it is critically important to let them know that you are taking a break, not ignoring them. After your break, make good on your word and go back to deal with the issue. If this is an altercation with a stranger (like the jerk in line at the store who's being rude), stop engaging in conversation and remove yourself as quickly as possible. Does it matter that this stranger is a jerk? No. It does not.

APPLY THIS: When you notice yourself getting revved up with anger, take a moment away from the conflict. Say something like, "This is too upsetting for me right now; I need a break," or, "I'm too angry to talk; I will be back in twenty minutes." Give yourself an out and get out. After you have cooled off, then you can go back and resolve the issue if you need to. Walk away at that moment so you can retain control over your emotions, and then you can decide if it is an issue that needs a solution or just something you don't need to engage in.

PART II:

FIND YOUR CENTER

Now that we have taught you some skills to manage some of the less pleasant emotions, let's expand out and deal with some of the stressors that arise from interacting with the world. After all, life has an endless supply of curveballs that it lobs at us, typically at inopportune times.

It is cracking me up right now that as I write the intro to the section about how to manage typical life stressors, I am getting the opportunity to practice what I preach. I am unexpectedly writing, not at my comfy desk with yummy snacks and nice music. Nope. I'm three hours into unexpectedly writing in the waiting room at the car dealership. My best-laid plans of writing in peace at home were interrupted by real life in the form of an unexpected electrical failure in my car. I have been invited to apply my own advice about lightening up, staying calm in the face of changed plans, and making the best of a moment that I wouldn't have chosen for myself.

How does a person feel happy when their day has been upended? How do you lighten up when you have a day where it feels like life is stacked against you? What can you do when you aren't getting what you want, and things feel like a hassle? In short, the question is, how can we be flexible in the face of things happening in ways we hadn't anticipated?

The flexibility of response and the ability to clearly understand and respond appropriately to life's curveballs is one of the critical skills we want our brains to develop. This is the result of more psychological flexibility: you are more nimble, and you work with reality instead of fighting it.

This section assists you in creating that flexibility we need so much. First, it gives you tips on how to lighten up when life is throwing those curveballs. Then we discuss the overall concept of happiness and give you actionable ways to increase your experience of our most sought-after emotion. Third, communication is handled because how much easier is life when you can effectively talk to the other people experiencing it with you? Finally, we discuss ways to actively manage some of the life hassles that can arise, plus (bonus) ways to avoid some of that stuff in the first place.

Life is stressful. The more flexibility you have, the easier it can be to dance right around the more common stressors, and the better you can manage the big dog issues that arise inevitably. Once you get rid of the idea that everything will go smoothly (always) and replace it with a mindset where you expect a certain amount of the unexpected, you can field a variety of unpleasant experiences elegantly.

CHAPTER 4:
LIGHTEN UP

TACTIC #30
LABEL THAT EMOTION

I WAS WORKING ON this very book, this chapter, in fact, when I found myself "visiting" the kitchen several times. Next, I found myself changing out laundry, and suddenly I decided I *had* to organize my daughter's old toys for a donation. In the middle of a handful of chocolate chips (this was after two handfuls of cheese crackers and some crummy, stale pretzels—you get the picture), I stopped myself. "Ah," I realized, "I'm anxious."

I slowed myself down enough to feel what was going on in my body (my stomach a little twisted, breathing a bit shallow, I felt tense in my chest), my thoughts (*Is this going to be good enough?*), and my behavior (noshing at that level almost always equals anxiety for me), and then figured out what was behind all this ridiculous procrastination. Once I figured out what was happening, I was able to sit down, pop in some gum, take a deep breath, and start typing.

This is a classic example of what psychologists teach in Acceptance and Commitment Therapy (my favorite model for my work).[7] If we can get more present and engaged with what is going on, then we can be more flexible in responding. One great place to start is to tune into our bodies. For example, someone might not catch that they are angry until they recognize the flush of heat spreading up their neck. After you have noticed what is going on in your body, then take a peek at the thoughts that are swirling and the emotions rising inside you.

How can you make this work for you? Slow down and pay attention to yourself. Ask questions and play detective: How are you behaving? What actions are you engaged in? What are the thoughts behind your actions? Is there negative self-talk going on? Thinking critical, distancing thoughts about someone else? How is your body feeling now? What emotion(s) is driving all this? Once you have the feeling labeled and the rest of the parts identified, you have more power to shift your thoughts, relax your body, and choose a more effective response, all of which can decrease the intensity of your emotion(s).

APPLY THIS: Take a moment to stop whatever weird, stressed out, or funky thing you are doing and take a breath. Then ask yourself, *What am I thinking?* Scan your body for areas of tension, tightness, discomfort, or funny sensations. Check out if you are behaving strangely (like my sudden rush to the kitchen nine times in a row). Ask yourself, *What feeling or feelings am I experiencing?* Scan through the typical thoughts, feelings, and body sensations you experience, so you can quickly identify patterns and get yourself unstuck.

TACTIC #31
ANTI-SUPERMODEL BREATHING

I DON'T KNOW IF many men have this problem but ask just about any woman out there, and she will likely, sheepishly admit that she walks around sucking in her belly all day. Now while this may help our waistlines appear marginally slimmer, it is a terrible idea for our breathing. Now, you guys out there, I know you don't necessarily hold your breath to try to look skinny, but I have seen a fair number of you tensing through your chest and breathing in that same shallow way. Male or female, when you are feeling strong emotions, one of the easiest, most effective, portable, and discreet ways to help yourself settle down is to breathe properly.

Breathing from our bellies is a terrific way to increase oxygen to our brains, increase circulation through our bodies, slow down, and help better decisions be made. Here is the basic formula:

More oxygen = Better thought clarity.

To get the most from your breath, you want to fill your lungs to capacity and then use the full force of your diaphragm to push out all the air. This requires that your belly moves out on the inhale, back in again on the exhale. Note that this is *not* that strange thing we do when we're overly nervous and take a huge breath, moving our shoulders like we're trying to throw a mountain off them. With belly breathing, your upper body mostly stays still, but your belly and chest expand and contract with the breath.

HERE WE GO: Relax your belly and place your hand there. Now imagine settling your shoulders *way* deep down from your ears. (When we get tense, we tend to shrug our shoulders. Like sucking in our bellies, this limits our lungs' range of motion.) Inhale. Feel your belly fill, and then your chest rise. Remember, your shoulders shouldn't move much since your torso is doing the work here. Inhale for a count of three. Hold for one to two seconds at the top, and then exhale, feeling your belly contract, also for a count of three. Repeat. Try it again a few more times. Set up a reminder system to repeat through the day. Stoplights? Breathe. Crummy boss walking down the hall? Breathe. Is kiddo having *another* tantrum? Breathe.

TACTIC #32
UPGRADE ME TO A BIGGER STOVE

IT'S A WEIRD truth about life that trying to do everything immediately decreases your chances of doing anything well. This is why one of the things I talk about with my clients all the time is setting their priorities.

A while back, there was an idea circulating on the internet that family, friends, health, and work make up our metaphorical four-burner stove. I don't know about you, but I've always chafed at limits, plus I love to cook and have always dreamed about having a double oven and a six-burner stove. (You know the one with the four burners on the side and the awesome griddle in the middle? Yeah, that one.) When I started thinking about this four-burner theory, I decided I needed an upgrade, and I chose the top six aspects of life I wanted to prioritize. Currently, the six include parenting, love/relationship, work, health, book, and friends/family (I put all those terrific folks in one big section).

Now is it realistic for me to give all six areas my complete attention all the time? Absolutely not. And to get things done like keeping my business in a good place while also writing my book, being a single mom, keeping fit, and enjoying my relationships, means that I am cutting corners occasionally or do a little less in one arena while I prioritize another. What does this look like, really? Well, it looks like instead of taking leisurely, long hikes every week, I do quick walks or gym workouts most days and do a day-long hike monthly. It means we make healthy nutrition choices, but we eat out. A lot. It looks like seeing my friends in groups for a while (like a big dinner party, see, I really do need that stove) while I take my other free time and pour it into writing. Stuff like that.

I am trimming where I can so I can focus on a broad array of priorities. At other times, it means leaving a few burners empty and going deeper into a few priorities instead of having all six categories filled. There is no right answer here, just your answer, in this unique season of your life. Maybe one of your priorities is playing golf; maybe you wouldn't dream of combining family and friends into one group, maybe four burners is plenty of burners for you.

APPLY THIS: If you are feeling overwhelmed by all that life demands, take a moment and see how you can divide life into four to six main categories that require your time and attention. Set up your "life stove" and prioritize the burners. For most of us, we *must* have one burner dedicated to health or personal wellness since if you're not taking care of yourself, the whole enterprise collapses. Then most of us need to account for work and for relationships, whether romantic, personal, or family.

Whatever your categories, these are the areas of focus for your life. It is helpful to then determine the day-to-day activities that make up the category. For example, if family is one of your priorities, then you need to carve out time with the kids and call your aunt Sally, stuff like that. Identify the top priorities, be honest about the habits that go with them, and give yourself permission to reallocate your energy or cut corners when needed. You got this.

TACTIC #33
ACCEPT THE INEVITABILITY OF CHANGE

WHAT A PARADOX life is. On the one hand, everything seems much the same, most of the time. Then, just as you are prepared for the predictable, things change. Both things, sameness and change, are happening every moment. This is why, by the way, therapy is such a neat experience; as a therapist, I get to work with a person's basic nature and also help them change.

The tricky thing about change is that we often want to predict how things will go for us. The more attached we get to a particular outcome, the harder it is when we are handed a different result than the one we wanted. This applies to the big things in life and the little stuff.

Here's a little example: Ever been out to eat and you find the perfect thing on the menu for dinner? You order, sure of what you want, and then the waiter returns, apologetic because they are out of your dish. It can ruin a dinner if you are unable to let go of your attachment to your original order. Because that one entree seemed like the *perfect* meal for this moment.

Now bigger changes occur all the time too: Jobs change, friends move away, loved ones die, and dreams don't come true. These changes are the tough ones to swallow. All these events, even the big, super unpleasant ones, are easier to manage if you can accept the inevitability of change. This helps you decrease your attachment to a desired outcome and to increase acceptance of the real outcome. This doesn't mean you won't grieve your losses, despair over dreams that don't work out, or struggle with situations that feel unexpected, unfair, or otherwise unwanted. It will help you spring back on your feet sooner and try out new opportunities in the face of the change you are experiencing. Remember, acceptance doesn't mean approval; it means acknowledging reality as it is.

APPLY THIS: When something isn't working out, change is coming your way, or your desired outcome is not happening, let yourself notice your disappointment. Breathe and acknowledge how you wanted things to go. Then challenge yourself to be realistic about how things are going. Notice what is in front of you and think about accepting the change. Talk to yourself about change being normal and assure yourself that you can handle the situation just fine. Breathe. Accept and move forward.

TACTIC #34

THIS IS EXACTLY WHAT I NEED RIGHT NOW (EVEN IF IT FEELS SO, SO WRONG)

One of my long-term clients is, shall we say, a little hotheaded. She is strong-willed and super smart, wickedly funny, and an incredibly loving, generous person. One thing she is not, however, is incredibly patient/calm/meek when angry. She has, on occasion, gotten into a couple of situations where she has ended up looking like the bad guy because she tends to lose her cool when pushed to her limit. Now, this is unfortunate because she rarely loses her cool except when someone else is truly in the wrong, but people often react most to the person who makes them feel uncomfortable and less strongly to the person at fault.

We were talking one day, and I shared with her a new mantra I had picked up along the way and used liberally, both with clients and in my own life. The mantra? "This is exactly what I need right now." The fun part of this mantra isn't using it when you're all Zen and calm already; *no*, that would be too easy. This works best when you use it because you are already halfway to furious.

Stuck in traffic on your way to a critically important meeting? Getting *super* peeved at the people moving like snails when you have somewhere you *need* to be? Ahh, breathe and think, *This is exactly what I need right now.* Now when your brain responds, *Yeah, like #@*& I need this right now*, you breathe and repeat the words, "This is exactly what I need right now," until you have calmed down. Say them out loud if you have to; repeat until the hostile thoughts in your head settle down a little.

Interestingly, when you calm down, you can often see that the situation you were *sure* you didn't need may have led to something good at the end (unheard of front row parking you would have missed if you'd been ten minutes early). Relaxing in that moment, especially when you don't have any control anyway, makes the most of the moment.

APPLY THIS: Next time life is handing you something you don't especially want, notice your desire to resist the situation. Notice how much you want to force a change or want to make something work out differently. Then, breathe and repeat the phrase, "for whatever reason, this is exactly what I need right now." Ignore the voice in your head screaming at you that you definitely *don't* want this right now, and simply repeat the phrase until you have calmed down a little. This is exactly what you need right now, even if it doesn't feel like what you need at all.

TACTIC #35
THE RULE OF FIVE

One of the things I see most often in my therapy practice is folks coming in *convinced* they know another person's motivation for some egregious behavior. Frequently, they have assumed that the other person is somehow *personally* against them and being intentionally disrespectful and rude. Here is where the Rule of Five applies. Basically, we are often skewed by our own self-importance and forget to think about any other perspectives to a problem. The Rule of Five is simple. When you are feeling quite stuck on an explanation of someone's behavior, you challenge yourself to think of five *different* reasons they are responding like this.

Ever been cut off in an important work meeting when making a brilliant point in front of your boss? Feeling super annoyed? Sure, the other person is doing this *on purpose, just to annoy you?* Well, that is one possible interpretation. Let's apply the Rule of Five:

1. He is doing this on purpose, to me personally, because he is a huge jerk.

2. He's competing with me again to look good in front of the boss.

3. Maybe he is nervous in big groups and talking to feel more in control.

4. Lack of impulse control? Maybe.

5. (And because it's good to make yourself giggle sometimes) The aliens made him do it.

Ever been brushed off by someone you care about? Feeling hurt by this and assuming they are either mad at you or blowing you off? Let's think about five possible options:

1. She is mad at me.
2. She is ignoring me on purpose because she doesn't care.
3. Maybe she is sick and not up to calling.
4. Maybe an emergency came up.
5. Maybe she is worried I am mad at her and is afraid to call, so I should reach out.

Once the assumptions are out of the way, you can either relax and give someone the benefit of the doubt, or you can reach out and determine where someone is coming from before your assumptions lead you down an incorrect path. Overall, your mission here is to avoid jumping to conclusions and limiting yourself to one or two negative thoughts about something. Rather, by pushing yourself to see five different options, you can see a broader perspective and make clear choices about how to proceed.

APPLY THIS: When you are feeling sure of someone's behavior and feeling hurt or mad about it, check in to see if you have all the information or are making assumptions. If you are making assumptions, try to get yourself to imagine five possible reasons this could be happening. Let your five range from the silly (abducted by aliens) to the serious (something is going on for them that I don't know about) and move forward from there.

TACTIC #36
YOU WANT THE PRESENT

ONE OF THE faulty thought patterns I see most often in my office is people's tendency to swing between the past and the future, with little tolerance for accepting their present situations. While I strongly believe in learning from the past, living in the past robs us of our present moments. Similarly, although I am a strong proponent of aspirations, I believe living too much in the future increases anxiety and is counterproductive to those same aspirations. Hence, we focus on increasing connection to the present.

Let's start with the past. I can't tell you how many times clients come in stuck in their pasts. Now, I must say I tend to work with folks who have quite a few past negative, traumatic experiences, so I am certainly not blaming these folks for feeling limited by What Has Been. However, waking up in the present and thinking to yourself *I can't change jobs because I never finished college*, or *All of my boyfriends have always abused me so I can't date now*, or *I've used alcohol since I was twenty years old so I can't ever stop*, is incredibly, incredibly destructive to present functioning.

All those past issues may have followed you into the present, but you certainly have the power to shift and change their current impact on your life. Let's go back to school, process your trauma history, learn about healthy relationships, or join a substance abuse program. Improve your present instead of remaining stuck in your past by figuring out action steps to repair the past and move forward.

Now to the future. How often do you think to yourself that you will be happy when you lose ten pounds, move to San Francisco, never have to see that terrible boss again, be noticed by that hot guy/girl, change careers, blah, blah, blah? Many of us are limiting our present functioning by making assumptions that our life will improve later once something is radically different. The problem here is, of course, that we are discounting what is happening now and waiting until some imagined time in the future to feel better. No matter how desirable those future realities might look, they can also be regarded as "my list of excuses for why I can't feel good now," dressed up as "goals," or even worse, "needs."

APPLY THIS: We can stop lamenting our pasts and wistfully wishing for our futures by improving our awareness and acceptance of our present reality. First, ask yourself whether you are more stuck in the past or the future. Next, ask yourself what you are willing to do, now, today, this week, to take one step toward improving your present. If you tend to be a person feeling trapped by your past, you often will need some support and healing to move forward. If you are a person feeling miserable in the present because something in the future hasn't happened yet, it is often helpful to take one small step toward that future while you improve acceptance of where you are, right now. Figure out your action steps and then repeat, repeat, repeat.

TACTIC #37
CHANGE SOMETHING, ANYTHING!

Jordan came into my office dejected and depressed. He was bummed about friends at school, his grades were slipping, and his parents were all over him for not performing well. The girl he had a crush on just started dating his best friend and a girl he didn't even like was chasing him around the school. He didn't feel good, played too many video games, and lived off quadruple espressos for energy. His hygiene left a lot to be desired, and his clothes were messy and rumpled. His shoulders were down, there wasn't any eye contact, and he slumped on the couch, complaining about how sucky his life was.

As we started talking, it was exceedingly difficult to help Jordan out of his gloom to even talk about anything meaningful. We were stuck in our session because depression was running the show. What happened next? Well, I asked Jordan to please stand up. I stood up with him. We stretched. We did some neck rolls and shoulder shrugs (pull shoulders up on purpose, then release, repeat a couple of times). I had him stretch his arms across his body and then hug himself. I had him change chairs, identifying that my seat was the power position, and encouraged him to think of it as such as he sat down there. Then we talked about what was and was not working in his life and built our therapy session from there.

Think about the many things you do *exactly the same way every time you do them*. When you're upset, do you cross your arms across your chest? Going into the conference room where you always sit on the second chair on the left? When you hear someone with different

Chapter 4: Lighten Up

political views, do you automatically start thinking about how wrong they are? I wonder what would happen if you changed something up? Made a different move, expressed a different opinion? Held your tongue when you might normally go off? It doesn't matter if you change something large or small, but changing something (*anything*) can help give you a fresh perspective.

APPLY THIS: Next time you have the chance, change at least one habit and see if it helps change your perspective. Now, this doesn't mean you won't be upset, or bored in the work meeting, or frustrated with someone's ideology, but you may get enough of a change to make a difference. If your current moment is poisoned by a terrible mood, it can help to shift your body and mind *enough* that you'll start to experience a shift in that difficult emotion. Start small, such as simply adjusting your posture or switching your chair. Notice your typical reaction and challenge yourself to do something different in that moment. Give yourself permission to not repeat the same habit/pattern/reaction you always do. Try something different and see how it opens new perspectives for you moving forward.

TACTIC #38
DO A FULL SENSORY VISUALIZATION OF YOUR HAPPY PLACE

Most of us have heard that we need to "visualize our goals," and so we dutifully, occasionally, think about what we want. However, this one-dimensional thought is rarely the rich, internal experience that is truly motivational over the long term. Thinking *I need a vacation* is not nearly as strong as a full-fledged, sensory experiencing of your ideal trip. In a full sensory visualization, you put together all the sights, sounds, smells, tastes, tactile sensations, and emotions associated with your ideal vacation. Here is the difference:

1. Basic thought: *I need a vacation.*
2. Full sensory visualization: *I see myself taking off eight days over the holidays and going to Maui. I want to stay in a comfortable condo and have a porch overlooking the ocean. I see myself in the kitchen fixing a delicious breakfast and I have towels warming in the dryer for my trip to the pool. I can smell the ocean and taste the fresh papaya as I start my morning relaxing with my partner, my feet on his lap as we share the paper and a fresh pot of coffee. I feel happy and content here.* (Want to go yet? I sure do.)

APPLY THIS: Prepare a full sensory visualization of your happy place. Then you can use this when you are feeling emotionally distressed and need to settle yourself down. Your visual can be of a place you have gone or somewhere you dream of going. It can be somewhere you plan to go in real life or just a happy place for you to go in your mind. Here are some questions to get you started:

Where do you want to go?

Visual: What does it look like? What can you see? Describe the colors, shapes, and things you see. Do you see yourself alone or with others?

Auditory: What can you hear? Are the sounds loud and energizing or more quiet and soothing? Is there music or laughter?

Taste: Are you eating anything? Is there anything you taste? What yummy thing are you looking forward to having?

Smell: What can you smell? How is it a different smell than where you are now?

Touch: How about tactile sensations? Is there a soft couch you are sitting on? Wind in your hair? The feel of your favorite pet under your hand? Holding hands with a favorite person?

Feelings: How do you feel emotionally?

Is there anything you need to add to your visualization to make it complete? Imagine it in vivid detail and enjoy returning to it whenever you need a little boost.

TACTIC #39
LEARN TO MEDITATE
* A GOING DEEPER TIP

MEDITATION ISN'T JUST for Buddhist monks anymore. There is a growing body of evidence that demonstrates meditation can *decrease* both anxiety and pain and *increase* happiness, mental clarity, immune functioning, and better overall emotional regulation. Meditation helps you achieve a clear, alert mind while separating you from your thoughts. Meditation does not have to be associated with any religious tradition, although many include it as a part of recommended spiritual practice. You do not need any fancy equipment, funny-smelling incense, funky cushions, or a chant in Sanskrit to meditate successfully. Rather, all you need is either a chair or another comfortable seat (I like legs crossed on the floor with a pillow underneath me) and two to forty-five minutes.

At a terrific conference I attended with Jack Kornfield[8] (famous Buddhist psychologist), he had us all rolling with laughter as he described meditating one day after he had been incredibly angry and the labeling of his thoughts as they came up: "Killing, killing, death, death, anger, anger." He told the story with good humor to illustrate that even those who have years of practice with meditation can have unpleasant or difficult thoughts arise. And the process is the same, whether the thought is of euphoric happiness, deep rage, or your grocery list: you notice the thoughts and move back to the breath. The overall goal is to let your thoughts pass through your mind, like clouds in the sky, without building a big story around them. Relax, enjoy, and try to do it daily, even if for five minutes. You will be surprised at how much difference those few minutes make once you practice with some consistency.

HERE ARE SOME TIPS TO GET STARTED: First, place yourself in a comfortable position. Rest your hands gently in your lap or on your knees. Relax your face, jaw, shoulders, and body. Take a few deep breaths. Now sit and focus on your breathing. You can count them if you'd like, one for an in-breath, two for the out-breath. Focus on that natural, instinctive process of breathing. When thoughts arise (as they will, a lot, especially at first), you can notice them and let them go. You can label the thoughts if you like ("ah, thinking") or the process behind them ("oh, revenge"). Just notice them briefly and return to your breath. When you get an urge to fix your body, you can shift it and move back to the breath, or notice the desire and sit with it, breathing all the while.

CHAPTER 5:
FEEL HAPPIER TODAY

TACTIC #40
THE 20 PERCENT SOLUTION

SEVERAL YEARS BACK, I took a business course led by the entrepreneurial guru Eben Pagan, who had us do a remarkable homework assignment. He asked us to shed 20 percent of our stuff. Yep, 20 percent of books, toys, kitchen stuff, clothes, furniture, you name it. He made it a "bonus exercise" to eliminate 20 percent of your debts or liabilities. Now the purpose of this exercise was to challenge the consumerism that drives us and to help us make room physically and financially in our lives.

I started thinking about the exercise and talked it over with some friends and clients, and we decided we could take it one step further and make it relevant to our minds by removing 20 percent of old negative stories we tell over and over, let go of 20 percent of our negative assumptions about others, eliminate 20 percent of our bad habits, and/or discard 20 percent of the bad things we think about ourselves.

The concept of letting go increases freedom. It is the opposite of our fear-based desire to gather, hoard, and keep everything the same all the time, which is, of course, both impossible and stressful.

What would you like some freedom from?

I know when I did this exercise, it was exciting to let go of several projects I had held onto, thinking I would get to them. Someday. When things were easier. Now I had thought, many times, about getting to them but had no real drive to make an attempt, and I had this nagging guilt about having the projects hanging around, incomplete.

How lovely it was to *decide* to let them go and then to *choose* to spend my time on other things. How refreshing to just *give up* the guilt and all its boring friends hanging around my head and heart.

A close friend of mine said, "I have decided it is time to give up my son's traumatic birth story; it's years later, and he is healthy now. I am going to let other mothers tell me their birth stories without me traumatizing them with mine. I can just focus on how great my son is now." A client said, "I am tired of my video games. I find myself not even enjoying playing them, but I spend hours at a time buried in the games anyway. I think I'm going to disconnect the system for a month and see if I like my life better."

APPLY THIS: Go through your house, your files, your office, your car, your thoughts, and your habits. Do you have 20 percent dragging you down in either internal or external environments? Holding onto things requires energy, while letting things go is freeing if you give yourself permission to let them go. Set aside some time, call the donation center, log into eBay or Craigslist, and sell some stuff, retire old stories, write it down, and tear up the old memories. Just get it out, out, out.

TACTIC #41
THOMAS JEFFERSON IS TIRED OF YOU CHASING AFTER HAPPINESS

I TOOK AN INFORMAL poll the other week of my clients, colleagues, and friends about what made them happy in the past week. The answers themselves didn't shock me, but the similarity of the answers was indeed surprising. Here are some of the most common answer categories:

- Getting outside/enjoying beauty:
  "I got to hike with my dog this weekend; it was awesome."
  "I went skiing today, the snow was horrible, but it was great to be outside."
  "I walked around the art museum. There were some beautiful pieces."
- Connecting with loved ones:
  "My boyfriend and I stayed home, made a frozen lasagna, and watched '90s movies."
  "My dad was in town; it was so nice to be with him."
  "I took the time on Sunday to just spend an afternoon painting with my child."
- Successes/accomplishments:
  "I made myself get out of the house today even when I didn't feel like it."

"I paid off my debt leftover from my divorce; what a relief."

"I got my paper turned in on time."

- Simple pleasures:

"I got my favorite type of coffee and brew it at home each morning."

"I finally adopted a kitten."

"I read a book just for fun."

Did you know the original definition of the word *pursuit* was to practice something? Not to chase after it, but to practice it over time. I am betting this was the definition our forefathers were using when they made the "pursuit of happiness" one of the inalienable rights of a United States citizen. Unfortunately, in our modern-day pursuits, we often chase after happiness instead of practicing it. The stories that the folks above tell show them *practicing* things that make them happy. One approach is to *make the decision* that being happy is important to us. And then to *choose happiness*, to put into play the actions that move us toward feeling happy more often. Whether you're an American or not, take advantage of that inalienable right.

APPLY THIS: Identify the small things, activities, and people in life that bring you happiness. Note that these are best accomplished with the things, talents, attributes, and relationships you currently possess. You will generally be disappointed in your quest for happiness if you are limiting yourself by only believing you will be happy ten pounds thinner, with a better mate, or after making a million dollars. Be happy now with what you can access and with the realistic interests in your life. The simple stuff works great and is easy to pursue over time.

TACTIC #42
LAUGHTER IS WHERE IT'S AT

One of the highlights of my day is going to the gym in the morning and having this adorable older couple tell me their joke of the day. Now, most of the time, they are real groaners. Like, "Why was the turkey arrested?" (Told, of course, during the holidays.) "He was suspected of foul play," ba-dum-bump. Eyeroll. The funny thing (pun intended) is that it makes people giggle. And then, on the better joke days, you hear other gym-goers telling each other the jokes. The day starts out with humor, along with the hard work. It's a lovely start to the day.

Remember the old saying about laughter being the best medicine? It has some merit. Folks who laugh often tend to have better immune systems, get sick less, and get healthy faster than those who report they laugh less.

If you spend any time around little kids, you will notice that they laugh all the time. Big, deep belly laughs, many times a day. They giggle; they even snort. When was the last time you laughed so hard you snorted? When was the last time you let yourself giggle or belly laugh? Ever been breathless, almost losing control over your bladder because something was so funny? I hope it was recently; it is terrific for you. It feels great to let go, let something tickle your fancy, make you smile, giggle, chortle.

So, once again, the trick here is to *consciously choose* laughter, humor, fun. Watch silly TV and humorous movies, read a funny book, listen to jokes, roll down a hill with a kid and laugh, laugh, laugh instead of worrying about messing up your hair. Hang out with your friends and tell stories about the funniest times each of you can remember. Recite *Monty Python* lines (yes, I am dating myself here). Think about your most embarrassing moments and let yourself see the humor in them now, then giggle about it, share the memory, and giggle with someone else about it too. Try to make it a regular part of your life to laugh, enjoy the ridiculous parts of life, smile, and choose fun. There is great freedom when you let go of being so serious all the time. Enjoy!

APPLY THIS: Schedule in some humor. Ask a friend to whatever silly, funny movie is out there and go enjoy yourself. Stream something hilarious at home. Read the comics. Listen to the comedy channel on your radio in the car. Make having fun and laughing a priority in your day. Be like the couple at my gym—look up jokes daily and spread the fun. Let yourself laugh.

TACTIC #43
PRESS REFRESH

ONE OF THE reasons we end up feeling miserable is when we feel stale, stuck, and bored. This is the opposite of feeling light, interested, and cheerful. Pursuing things that are interesting, fresh, and new have an incredible way of brightening our outlook. When was the last time you went to a conference? Learned something new? Pursued a new interest?

When life gets serious, as it often does, we tend to let go of exploring. Somehow paying bills and meeting responsibilities gets in the way of discovery. Let me help you claim back some of that wonder.

First, make a list of all the things that are interesting to you. Now, it is critically important to make this list as if *any* of the things on it are possibilities. Don't fret at this point that you are not tall enough, rich enough, old enough, young enough, thin enough, smart enough, etc. Just make the list, not holding anything back. This means you write down everything that comes to mind before your mind goes, "But?" Okay, go.

Got your list? Great. Okay, now let's look at it. Want to live overseas and travel the world but have a job that ties you to a certain city? Curious about astrophysics (or any other super complex subject)? No worries. No matter what, there are themes and patterns to the things you find interesting, and you can start small, read about them, take a lesson, schedule a trip, something that gets to the essence of your interest. In many cases, only our fearful assumptions about trying something new hold us back. Once you give yourself permission to start at the beginning of your interest, you can often enjoy some success and then decide if it's something you want to continue to pursue.

Chapter 5: Feel Happier Today

Here's a fun example. My mother, who is a smart, tiny, elegant woman, also has a heavy right foot. She loves to drive and always jokes about missing her calling as a race car driver. Now, this is a highly unlikely dream to come true at this point (she is in her seventies), but my brother and I figured she could at least get a taste of her dream, so a while back, we arranged for her to take a test drive on a real racetrack. She got to suit up, climb through a window into a race car, and zoom around for a while. It was fun for her to do and fun for us to watch her do. Remember, allowing yourself to be curious and try things is the point; becoming the next Dale Earnhardt isn't (even if you wish you could).

 Use the worksheet on the next page to help yourself figure out how to refresh your life. Pick a big dream or desire and break it down into more realistic parts. Have fun letting yourself think about what you want, and then figure out how to make small steps in that direction.

PRESS REFRESH WORKSHEET

Use this space to list out your dreams, interests, things you would pursue if you had nothing holding you back. Disregard reality here; list the ideal scenario(s).

For example, I want to live on a ranch in Belize and raise horses for a living.

_____

_____

_____

_____

_____

_____

_____

_____

_____

_____

_____

_____

_____

Use this space to get a little closer to reality. What are the themes of your ideal list above? What is it that you want or need more of in your life?

For example, I need beach time and to be around horses more often.

_____

_____

_____

_____

_____

_____

_____

This is your action list. Take the themes above and make some part of it happen today, this week, or sometime soon.

For example, start saving for a beach vacation and schedule riding lessons.

_____

_____

_____

_____

_____

_____

TACTIC #44
SING, DANCE, AND BE SILLY

When I was nineteen years old, I couldn't figure out my college major. To help me figure things out, I took a test that looked at a variety of aptitudes. The test basically confirmed that I liked to think (a lot), liked helping people (a lot), and suggested fields such as law or psychology for a career. Great news since I had long wanted to be either a lawyer or a psychologist.

On a less positive note, the test also revealed that I scored as low as they had seen anyone, ever, in the history of the test, score on the ability to distinguish tones and sounds. I am certifiably tone-deaf. Now, this is not so much of a problem for me, as I sound totally fine to myself. Feedback from others, however, suggests that my sound is not so sweet.

Since I don't like feeling embarrassed or making others uncomfortable, this little issue caused me to stop singing. So imagine my resistance when I took a course[9] on happiness and joy, and one of the homework assignments was to sing as often as I could muster. The theory behind the assignment is that singing is joyful, and causes good resonance in your brain, and connects you emotionally with something sensory. All great reasons, right? But how to get over my embarrassment and get around my terrible voice? Easy—I do it in the car. Now if you see me driving around Denver, I will likely be singing, loudly and badly, with a huge smile on my face. No harm done, and the guy who suggested I sing was right—it is fun and makes me happy.

Sometimes limiting yourself is truly important, but much of the time, I see myself and others limiting themselves for reasons of pride, importance, embarrassment, or fear of seeming silly. These types of limits, well, limit you. I wonder what self-imposed, unnecessary limits you might be able to let go of? I wonder what you might shed if you chose to care more about happiness than your dignity, or the opinion of others, or the ability to do something "well"?

APPLY THIS: Identify what limits you can release. Afraid to dance? Boogie down when you're at home by yourself. Scared to sing? Sing in the shower. Feel stiff and grouchy a lot? Make silly faces at the kids in the car in front of you who are making silly faces at you. Be ridiculous more often. Do things like dress up for Halloween, even if it is just for you to hand out candy. Sing, dance, be silly. On purpose. As often as you can.

TACTIC #45
STRIVE FOR GOOD

ONE OF MY clients came into my office the other day, concerned about her lack of perfection. She reported that she had done a presentation a few days prior to this high-powered women's group. While she felt the presentation had gone well overall and seemed to be well received, she became flooded with anxiety after she left. Had she been too sarcastic? Was the information too much in too little time? Why didn't she offer her business cards (even though the facilitator had distributed an agenda with her bio and information on it)? The summary of the concern: "Ugh—so much room for improvement."

What a great opportunity she presented to talk about the crippling nature of perfectionism. Gretchen Rubin, a famous author on the topic of happiness, calls perfection "the enemy of the good."[10] She warns, and I agree, that perfectionism is a happiness killer. It leaves you feeling lousy about yourself and your work, even when, like my client mentioned above, that work is good.

Basically, the pull of perfectionism is a trick. It makes you think you have to do something exactly right, without errors, better than anyone has ever done it before, before you can feel good enough about yourself to move forward. The problem with this line of thinking is that it typically keeps you from starting something at all, or if you can start, are often not able to finish. Perfectionism encourages you to procrastinate, leading to pushed deadlines, late submissions, or incomplete projects. The funny thing about all these outcomes is that they end up being far from perfect, often make you look bad, and certainly make you feel bad. Unbelievably bad. When perfectionism is indulged, not only is your product not perfect, but it will also often be late, incomplete, rushed, or not even attempted. How crummy.

Moving away from perfectionism involves giving yourself permission to do something good, okay, competent, complete. Maybe you will bump it up to excellent or great in the future, but to start, you have to go for acceptable.

Acceptable. Ewww. I know, it doesn't sound nearly as good as perfect. Doesn't sound nearly as desirable as excellent. Do it anyway. Be good, not perfect. Just get it started and edit later if it is a project. Get started and practice until you are a little bit better if it is a skill. Begin at the beginning and learn more if it is an intellectual pursuit. Just get started first, and then strive for pretty darn good instead of perfect.

APPLY THIS: Understand that perfectionism is exhausting for you and others around you. Instead of falling into the perfectionist trap, try to go for good enough. Take something you have been stuck on and take one step toward moving forward. Then try to figure out a way to improve it a tiny bit. Let yourself spend five minutes, and then five more; repeat until you have something good, decent, or gloriously acceptable. Give yourself a break from perfect.

TACTIC #46
WRITE A THANK-YOU LETTER

Who is the person who most influenced you growing up? How about the person who helped you in high school? Any coaches in college? How about that boss who believed in you at your last job and took you under their wing? How about the friend who helped you through your terrible breakup? Know someone who makes you smile every time you pick up the phone? Told your significant other lately how much they mean to you?

It is time to write a thank-you letter or maybe a couple of them. Being grateful helps you build those happy circuits in your brain (for more on this, see the tip coming up on keeping a gratitude journal). One way of expressing gratitude is to think about and then acknowledge those folks who have been influential to you along the way. If you can be thoughtful in your recollection and give specific examples, this solidifies the good feeling of gratitude in you, plus it makes the person on the receiving end fully understand how they helped you.

When a client reached out and asked me in between sessions how to feel less lonely, this was one of my suggestions. At that moment, especially when you're feeling isolated, acknowledging the contribution of others to your life can help you feel more connected, even if it was a person in the past. Expressing thanks to someone's influence in your life reminds you that you are not in this life alone and helps honor those connections that led you to become the person you are today. Not happy with who you currently are? This helps here too because it can remind you of someone who saw the best in you. Then you can take a few steps towards being that awesome person they thought you were.

APPLY THIS: Take a half-hour or so to think about a person who truly made a difference in your life. Now write them a letter answering some or all of the following questions. What did they do that was so meaningful? Can you remember anything in particular they said or did that hit home with you? How have you used their advice, suggestions, or teachings to forward your life? Is there anything you would like them to know about you now? Then say, "Thank you," and mail the letter. Savor that good memory and the nice feeling that comes from letting someone know how they have made a difference to you.

Bonus points in our age of electronic communications to handwrite this letter and mail it—you know, like with a stamp and envelope and everything. Handwritten communication is particularly impactful to our brains, both for the person who writes it and for the person who reads it.

TACTIC #47
LEARN SOMETHING NEW ALREADY

THIS TIP SPEAKS to our tendency as a species to be hard on ourselves. We have this idea that we should gain mastery over each new experience right away. Sometimes we even set ourselves up by not practicing and then expecting perfection on the first try (see perfectionism tip #45 for more about combating this nasty habit). However, what leads to more happiness and enjoyment is to try to judge performance on a series of attempts, a process of learning something over time, a gradual accumulation of skill.

I was working with a man who, at the age of sixty-one, wanted to learn how to snowboard. Now for those of you familiar with the sport, you know it's typically a younger persons' game because the learning curve, while short, is very steep. This means you can get good more quickly, say, than skiing, where the learning curve is gentler, but it takes a long time to get good. With snowboarding, you can often get some real expertise in just one season, but boy, those first ten days on the mountain are going to be hard. You fall, you fall again, you fall so much it is a good idea to wear wrist guards so you don't break your wrist.

So this guy goes out, and on his first day, he hangs in there and does pretty well, but at the end of the day, his snowboard slips out from under him on some ice. Crack—he gets a mild concussion. He feels frustrated, incompetent, and is hard on himself. He is reminded, however, that this is a process of learning. He is going to gain competence over time. It counts (quite a bit) that he took a risk to learn something so foreign. The last time I checked, he had persevered and had made the switch from skiing to boarding. Did I mention that he was on ski patrol? And was able after a season to switch to snowboard ski patrol? Pretty cool stuff.

The next time you are beating yourself up that you didn't get that something new "right," try to reframe the situation. Look at it from another angle. Give yourself credit for trying, for seeing what you can do to learn more, for gradually gaining competence over time. Try again and again. Enjoy the ride.

APPLY THIS: Think about something new you have been wanting to try or tried once and stopped pursuing because you weren't great out of the gate. How could you learn more about this activity? Any chance you could try it again? Take a peek at your weaknesses and see what new skill you might like to try. Resist the urge to quit in the beginning because you're no good. Recognize that the point of learning something new is the learning process. You start out not knowing something and, over time, with practice, improve. Give yourself a chance to learn something new.

TACTIC #48
DECREASE REGRET
*A GOING DEEPER TIP

THOUGHTS LIKE *I wish I had*, or *I wish I hadn't*, are true happiness killers. Regret eats away at you. Regret increases self-doubt and generally feeds negative thoughts about what you did wrong. Not so conducive for happiness.

The question is how to avoid accumulating regret in the first place? Basically, this involves a couple of things. First, it is being clear about your values. Values are not just the religious or spiritual or cultural rules and norms of your "people" (although these can also be important if they are yours as well) but also your *personal values*: those that help form your knowledge of yourself as a person and how you think you "should" act. (See tip #27.) Now, those of you who know me know that the word "should" is generally one I leave out of my vocabulary, but in this case, "should" can be useful in matching behavior to actions.

Second, avoiding regret is about taking opportunities when they arise. Have courage and take the leap when something new, exciting, or interesting comes your way. Don't think your way out of it. But do think about whether this opportunity matches up with your values—if so, act. Once you are clear it lines up with who you are, or who you want to be, go for it. Give yourself permission to take opportunities large and small when they come up.

Third, the recipe for less regret involves avoiding the things that you can guess beforehand will make you unhappy and regretful later. This is tricky because it means slowing down enough to put off short-term gain for a longer-term reward. Take the time to make sure you are choosing something with positive short- and long-term consequences.

The goal here is to think through your choices and weigh the short- and long-term rewards. Then choose based on your values, and what will lead to feeling good in the short and long run, decreasing regret.

Do take that offer to fly to London on a whim. *Don't* sleep with your married neighbor (even if he/she is the hottest person of all time). Say yes to the opportunity to learn how to play the piano like you always wanted. Avoid gossip. Be a direct communicator. Plan a designated driver when you go out. Don't fight. Say yes to a piece of cake, not the whole thing. Got it? Good. You'll feel great later that you had the forethought and courage to think through your choices.

TACTIC #49
KEEP A GRATITUDE JOURNAL
*A GOING DEEPER TIP

Feeling low? Finding yourself predicting that something bad is going to happen? Tired of seeing everything in a pessimistic light?

One of the reasons we get stuck on difficult thoughts and feelings is that these are the thoughts and feelings that tend to catch hold and refuse to let go. It is difficult to bully yourself into thinking or feeling differently (and it is generally awful to bully yourself anyway), but it is possible to subtly shift so you can notice the complexity of life, instead of just the stuff you don't like. One way to do so is to deliberately notice, savor, and share the positive thoughts, feelings, experiences, people, and events that occur in our lives.

We are looking to shift from a habit and pattern of thinking and feeling only the negatives to noticing and "preferencing" the lovely mixture of things in life.

Chapter 5: Feel Happier Today

HERE'S ONE WAY TO DO IT: Get yourself a nice blank book, a fancy journal, a Post-it note pad, or your favorite note-taking app on your electronic device. Then, schedule time to write down three things you appreciate in your day, every day, for twenty-one days in a row. They can range from the tiny, like noticing spring blooms on a tree, or the large, like getting a promotion. Just write about three things you felt happy about, proud of, made you giggle, made you smile, felt good, you're excited about—you get the idea. Be specific and try to challenge yourself to notice unique things each day and write them down. It is a more robust and effective exercise if you can be clearer and more detailed ("I closed the Smith company deal today") rather than general ("my life"). Your emotions and thoughts are more effectively engaged when you notice specifics as well as write them down, rather than just think about them for a second.

If you are having a super crummy day, sometimes we have to dig deep, and our gratitude journal looks like: "Tomorrow is a new day," or "I can still walk." Most days, it is easy, once you get into the habit of noticing the breadth of life, to find genuinely good things happening to write down. After the twenty-one days, take stock and notice if this is something you want to continue daily, every week, or periodically.

CHAPTER 6:
GET YOUR POINT ACROSS

TACTIC #50
PUT AWAY THAT POINTY FINGER AND LET'S TALK

Ever wondered what a contentious couples session sounds like? They typically start with what we in the therapy biz call "the pointy finger conversation." All the sentences start with words like: "You always," or "I can't believe you didn't," or "How many times have I told you?" Responses typically sound like "Well, I only do (insert offensive behavior here) because," or "But *you* told me that *you* wanted (X), so I did (X). How are *you* still upset about that?"

Do any of these phrases sound familiar? Do you notice each one is a variation on an accusation? Another common speech pattern in the pointy finger conversation is to command instead of ask. Statements like "You can't do that" or "You're going to listen to me" fall into this problem category. Unfortunately, accusations rarely create an effective resolution to conflicts. More times than not, when you start a conversation by attacking the other person, they tend to get defensive, and either clam up, stop listening, or return the hostility by fighting back.

You can test this with the classic move of accusing someone dear to you, out of the blue, of "being defensive" or asking, "Why are you so defensive?" Then, he or she has pretty much no choice but to respond, "What are you talking about? I'm not defensive." See? Defensive.

Move away from destructive confrontations and have a productive, constructive conversation instead. Using assertiveness instead of accusation can be an extremely helpful way to increase direct, clear communication and is based on the three main steps of assertive communication:

First, identify: *What is the problem?*

Second, identify: *How does this affect me?*

Third, identify: *What change do I want?*

Finally, put it all together with the assertiveness formula: I am feeling _____ because of _____ and I would like _____ to happen instead.

Let's practice: "It is upsetting to me when the house is a mess, and I would appreciate it if you could help me pick things up a little more" (new, assertive way) versus "You never take care of things around the house, I can't believe you are such a slob" (old, pointy finger way).

APPLY THIS: Next time you are about to start a conversation (confrontation) with a "you" based accusation, change to an "I" statement and use the assertiveness formula instead. Try saying, "I am feeling _____ because of _____ and I would like _____ to happen instead." Or you can change it up and say something like: "When _____ happens, I tend to feel _____ and I would prefer we do _____ instead." You get the gist: "I" statements, speak from your feelings, and talk about preferences instead of making accusations.

TACTIC #51
EMPHASIZE RESPONSIBILITY AND CONTRIBUTION INSTEAD OF BLAME

Do you remember playing pin the tail on the donkey when you were a kid? The basic concept is that you get blindfolded and spun around, and then you are supposed to pin on the donkey's missing tail. Generally, the kid ends up trying to pin the tail on Aunt Susie or cousin Sal, and everyone laughs and eventually points the kiddo in the right direction.

Finding someone to blame is a little bit like playing pin the tail on the donkey. Assigning blame is typically a response to feelings of uncertainty, shame, or worry that you are getting laughed at or picked on. Focusing on blame generally blinds you to the real complexity of a situation, and trying to figure out where to pin the blame is awfully tough when you can't see clearly because you are all spun around by conflicting emotions. Instead of relying on blame, a richer and more effective approach is to examine the various contributions each party brought to the problem situation.

The people at the Harvard Negotiation Project (you know they're smart) wrote a book called *Difficult Conversations*, where they talk all about this contribution solution.[11] In essence, the concept aligns with that old proverb, "It takes two to tango." In almost any situation involving a miscommunication, all parties involved contributed something to the problem at hand. If you accept this as true, yes, even in those situations where you are convinced of your own rightness, then you are one step closer to the solution.

A bonus to thinking through responsibility, rather than assigning blame, is that it changes our focus from fault to working on a solution to the problem. Talking about contributions to problems gets a much better response from others than telling someone it is their fault. A better understanding of the problem is achieved, a conversation between the parties is more likely to be productive, and the problem is (hopefully) easier to solve in the present moment as well as to avoid in the future.

APPLY THIS: Next time a problem has you frustrated, take a minute to identify how you might share responsibility and figure out a solution from a responsible stance versus a blaming one.

Original method: "I can't believe this project didn't get done right. James screwed this up. Why didn't he know better?"

New, assertive method: "Hmmm, this didn't turn out the way I anticipated. James took this in a different direction than I wanted. I wonder if I wasn't clear about my expectations; maybe he didn't get that last email detailing how to complete this. I guess I need to check with him to get a better understanding of what he heard and how we want to proceed from here."

TACTIC #52
FIRST SEEK TO UNDERSTAND, THEN BE UNDERSTOOD

Feeling peeved? Really steaming about something? First, take a minute to calm down, breathe, and relax your body. Then take a couple of minutes to figure out what just happened. Where is the other person coming from? Listen and listen well. Important note: "Listen" means *stop* doing that thing where you are trying to think about how to respond and coming up with a clever argument to knock down the other person's point of view. We tend to feel so certain about how someone is thinking or feeling, but we are often wrong about their motives. Seeking to understand often leads to major revelations.

Instead of jumping to conclusions, listen and ask questions to help you better understand the issue and the other person's perspective. Great ways to do this are questions like: "Tell me more," "I'm curious why you feel that way," and "Can you share more about how you came to that position?"

Then summarize what you have heard. "So, what I hear you say is X." Pause. Stop talking. Wait and see if they will confirm that you are hearing accurately. If you get feedback that you aren't getting their perspective, then ask for clarification. Try saying, "I'm not sure what you mean," or "Could you explain more about that?"

Be assertive (see tip #50 on the assertiveness formula earlier in this section), and use "I" statements instead of accusations. Like: "I have never thought of it that way," or "That is an interesting perspective" to let the other person know they have been heard, even if you don't agree with them. *Remember listening to someone and agreeing with them are two different things.* You can hear someone out and increase your understanding of where they are coming from without agreeing with them *at all*. Try to respect the other person's perspective, especially when you don't agree.

Approaching conversations and disagreements in this way increases understanding on both sides and leads to better listening and compromises than having the two sides of the story try to hammer the other with their point of view. Plus, even if an agreement isn't possible, both sides can at least feel respected and heard, which opens to better possibilities down the road.

APPLY THIS: In the middle of a tough conversation? Try the approach of listening and seeking to understand the other person's point of view. Ask questions to get more information, and then reflect on what you heard. If you don't get it the first time, ask more clarifying questions. If it is clear you won't agree, hear the other person out, and let them know you have heard them. Remember, listening and agreeing are two separate things. You can listen and hear someone and still not come to a consensus. Listening and understanding is a great place to start. An agreement can come down the line.

TACTIC #53
ASK WITH CURIOSITY

As a culture, we seem to reward the concept of "either/or." If you pay attention to the way the news (all kinds of news) is framed, it appears we are supposed to be consistently divided into one way of thinking or another. We should be a Republican or a Democrat, Liberal or Conservative, pro-this or anti-that. These positions of certainty and knowing, however, tend to polarize us, divide us, and distance us from one another.

There's the constant suggestion that if you believe in one thing, you certainly aren't permitted to believe in this other thing "across the aisle," and thus all things get divided into right and wrong—the only possible "right" being predetermined by each of the two rival camps. This sort of division encourages two groups to argue with one another rather than converse and understand.

We mimic this behavior in our relationships, with friends, neighbors, and partners, even with people on the street. We distance ourselves from others because they look different, sound different, or have a different opinion. We assume we are closer to someone who looks like us, votes like us, shops at the same grocery store. In some ways, these assumptions are correct, but in many ways, they are not. Adopting a stance of curiosity can help us better understand, empathize with, and engage in conversation with others who appear to be different than us.

In my work as a therapist, I get the unique opportunity to see folks from all walks of life. On a typical day, I have an amazing variety of clients, ranging from highly successful older adults to teens trying to figure out how to get started in the world. I see housewives, artists, contractors, executives, and folks with high-level security clearances.

Chapter 6: Get Your Point Across

My clients tell me secrets, and I am constantly struck by how similar people's stories are, despite the different professions, political opinions, appearances, and backgrounds. Being curious and not making assumptions helps me join with my clients and helps them feel heard, cared for, and understood.

Trying to be more open and curious about someone can lead you to learn new and wonderful things about someone else. Remember, you don't have to agree. You're just learning about someone's point of view. Listening and asking questions from a position of curiosity leads to richer, deeper conversations and increases closeness, even between people who are quite different. This type of approach is based on uncertainty, not-knowing, and curiosity, versus knowing, pushing your opinion, and moral rectitude. This allows a "both/and" version of interaction, which encourages coming together rather than an "either/or" distancing interaction.

APPLY THIS: Next time you are with someone you don't know or seems to have a different (therefore obviously "wrong") opinion, try asking them more about the differences. Be curious about how they came to hold that opinion and why it is important to them. Ask about where they think it is leading them and if it makes them happy. Ask how you can get along despite the difference of opinion. Ask, be curious, set aside your preconceived notions, and be open.

TACTIC #54
CARROTS ARE YOUR TICKET

INTERESTED IN CONFRONTING someone? Think they need to hear you out? Want them to agree with you now? Let me give you a hint. Telling them they are wrong is not likely to get you far. Even if they are wrong, rubbing their nose in it isn't going to do much to get them to acknowledge, admit, and deal with the problem. Remember, most folks want to be heard, understood, and accepted, even when they have messed up—especially when they have messed up.

Ever heard the saying that you attract more flies with honey than vinegar? Or maybe you have heard that the best way to motivate a donkey (notoriously stubborn animals) is to use a carrot, not a stick. Well, people aren't so far removed from the flies and donkeys of the world. As a species, we tend to react strongly to the "sticks" of life: criticism, rejection, displeasure. Pretty much all the neuroscience researchers would argue we are instinctually hardwired to avoid a threat before moving toward a reward. Sticks, unfortunately, are a more powerful motivator than carrots.

While we are hardwired to acknowledge and avoid a threat, we all tend to enjoy, warm to, and like being treated well. Most of us like to feel like we have gotten something right, made an impact, and are appreciated. And most of us will go out of our way to respond to someone who holds us in that light.

The next time you are trying to get someone over to your side, or wanting to motivate someone to hear you better, or do something for you, try the carrot approach. Instead of criticizing, try starting out with a positive comment, then provide constructive feedback. This is an especially valuable practice when parenting, or in any situation where you are higher on the hierarchy than the person you are dealing with. You're the boss, talking to an employee? A parent talking to a child? A friend teaching another friend how to do something? In each of these situations, a carrot is called for. Reward, compliment, encourage, support, and ask instead of criticizing, threatening, discouraging, telling, ordering, or commanding.

APPLY THIS: Try using the carrot approach when you need to motivate someone. Be encouraging and notice positives first. Compliment before you correct. Think of ways to reward someone as your primary method of motivation.

TACTIC #55
MISTAKES HAPPEN

WHAT IS IT about saying sorry that is so hard to do? Is it about making a mistake in the first place? Or is it about admitting you made a mistake? My guess is it is a nasty combination of both.

I don't know about you, but I have a well-developed relationship with perfectionism. Perfectionism and I have been close since I was a kid, and it seems to have followed me into adulthood. What are the characteristics of my relationship with perfectionism, you ask? Well, I hate making mistakes, hate when I can't do things right, and generally get down on myself when I mess up. All my training and most of my experience in life, however, tells me that perfectionism is a lousy thing to keep around. It makes me miserable and often keeps me from trying out something new. Remember, perfect easily becomes the enemy of good.

The solution to this seems to be to try harder, be flexible in trying new things, open my mind, and let go of control. Also, it helps to be honest, with myself and others, about the mistakes I make. Owning them, being straightforward about the effect they have, and apologizing quickly allows me to learn from them, to avoid becoming a repeat offender in that arena, and most importantly, to keep them from getting in the way of my friendships, partnerships, and relationships.

Here is the rub, though: admitting mistakes feels uncomfortable. Admitting you are wrong, have screwed up, or hurt someone's feelings brings up anxiety. This discomfort stops many people in their tracks, and they get defensive instead of admitting they are at fault. Take a deep breath and acknowledge the error to yourself first. Then, decide how to handle it.

THINK ABOUT THIS: Not every mistake needs to be publicly aired, but every mistake warrants learning from it so it doesn't happen again (or at least happens less often). First, admit your mistake, then see if there is an apology due or amends to be made. Get going on that apology, make those amends, learn from the mistake, and move on. Harboring anger and resentment toward yourself, beating yourself up, or talking down to yourself ("I'm so stupid; how could I have done that?") None of these will help the healing one iota. Let yourself admit the mistake, learn from it, strategize about how to prevent it from happening again, and make it right as best you can.

TACTIC #56
AVOID AVOIDANCE

Recently I was working with a young woman who was dating someone she knew wasn't "the one," but she kept avoiding breaking up with him because she didn't want to hurt his feelings. Another person I worked with had something major to tell his wife but was too afraid she would be mad, so he let a secret eat away at him rather than share it. Just the other day, I needed to tell a friend I couldn't get together, but I was afraid to call her because I had canceled the last time, and I didn't want to hurt her feelings or look like a perpetual no-show. All these stories have avoidance in common.

Typically, avoidance is motivated by a desire to avoid pain, either for ourselves or for someone else. We fear being judged, rejected, making someone angry, hurting someone, or not getting what we want. The problem with avoidance is that we are moving away from something we don't want but not closer to what we do want.

Have you ever had the experience where you know what you want to say but are afraid to say it? Do you then find yourself hemming and hawing, thinking but not verbalizing what you want? Are you doing something over and over you don't enjoy, just because you don't want to have to confront the issue? Worried someone will reject you if you say what you mean?

Saying what we mean directly and without shame is critical to success in communication. It is more honest and effective in the long run, even if it can be excruciating in the short term.

Chapter 6: Get Your Point Across

APPLY THIS: The next time you find yourself avoiding an important conversation, try the following strategies to be able to say what you mean.

First, acknowledge that you feel uncomfortable and are avoiding something (or someone).

Second, try to explore what you are avoiding. Are you afraid of hurting someone? Making them mad? Being a disappointment? Wanting a change but feeling scared?

Third, think about what it is you need to say, what issue you need to bring up or solve.

Fourth, *say what you mean*. Be clear. Let the other person know this is a hard thing to talk about. Ask them to listen so you can get your point across. Avoid avoidance and be direct.

TACTIC #57
FOCUS ON THE HERE AND NOW

Some of the least helpful words in communication are the biggest ones. "Never," "always," "every time," and "all the time" are typically thrown around in anger in heated conversations when things aren't going well. Past experiences, often from the distant past, are used as "proof" that someone "always" disappoints, or "never" comes home on time, that "every time we are out" something bad happens or they are drinking/working/sleeping "all the time." These are globalizations, small words making something true more often than not. The problem is this tendency to think of things as continuous, frequent, and forever tends to be flawed. We are often preferencing a negative story and ignoring a positive one in these moments, which leads to increased conflict.

Ever been in a disagreement with someone, and they say something like, "You're always late"? I would bet that your next response sounds something like "No, I'm not," and the conversation disintegrates from there. Global statements like "always" and "never" tend to cause people to react defensively. They are reacting to the accusation you have leveled at them, and have typically, at that point, stopped trying to hear what you are saying. If you use here and now words, using a fair accounting, you are more likely to get your point across, be heard and understood, and have the other person respond in a way that will lead to a resolution.

APPLY THIS: Here are some examples of taking global words and changing them into here and now words. The point is to be talking about something in the moment rather than bringing in past issues.

Old way: "You're always late."
New way: "It is frustrating to me to wait thirty minutes past our dinner reservation. It makes me feel embarrassed, and I also find myself worrying about if you are okay."

Old way: "You never take care of things around the house."
New way: "I would appreciate some help with the dishes today."

A variation on globalization is using name-calling words that pigeonhole someone into negative behavior. Instead of using name-calling to get someone to change, try being more specific about what you need. Check this out:

Old way: "You're such a slob."
New way: "I would appreciate it if you could pick up your laundry."

Making the shift from global, forever, name-calling type statements to action-oriented requests is likely to make a difference in your communication.

TACTIC #58
THE THREE WORST WAYS TO SOLVE A PROBLEM
* A GOING DEEPER TIP

PROBLEM-SOLVING CAN BE challenging. When faced with problems, we do best with assertive communication, where we try to honor our needs and the needs of someone else. We can slip into negative patterns when we aren't careful. The worst three ways to solve a problem are listed below. Ask yourself if you fall into any of these styles. Strive to change those patterns into a more assertive (and effective) style.

#1. AGGRESSIVE RESPONSES:

Attacking others with words, name-calling, put-downs, throwing things, or physically attacking others describes aggressive approaches. While aggression feels powerful, it diminishes compliance, builds resentment, and can lead to unpleasantries such as restraining orders. The hallmark of aggressive communication is meeting our own needs in such a way that the rights of others are violated. Typically, we use this response when we are motivated to dominate, control, get back at, or embarrass someone else. We are particularly at risk of using aggressive communication when we feel threatened. If someone is aggressive with us, it can be difficult to resist responding in kind. Often, we need to take a physical break from the situation, walk away, and regain perspective to avoid giving into aggressive impulses.

#2. PASSIVE RESPONSES:

Folks who use a passive approach are the ones who want to pretend there isn't a problem. They refuse to deal with conflict and may even go to the extreme of giving in, apologizing when it isn't their fault or otherwise try to ignore or avoid a problem. This is the ostrich-with-its-head-in-the-sand approach. It is generally ineffective and often backfires on you. Passive responses allow our rights to be violated, either by ignoring our own needs or by allowing other's rights to be more important. We are often led into passive responses when we are feeling threatened but less powerful than our aggressor. Under threat, the passive person tends to acquiesce rather than inflame the attacker. The problem with this approach is that it feeds the aggressor and disempowers the passive recipient, creating a vicious cycle of poor communication and victimization. Figuring out a way to handle the conflict rather than pretend it isn't there is critical.

#3. PASSIVE-AGGRESSIVE RESPONSES:

This is a particularly insidious way to solve a problem. The passive-aggressive person will say one thing and do another, agree, and then sabotage behind your back. Subtle get-even maneuvers can be expected in the passive-aggressive approach. This type of response is characterized by standing up for our rights in such a way that the rights of another are violated, but we pretend that this isn't occurring. The purpose here is to manipulate others and get what we want without being clear in our communication. We are often tempted to use a passive-aggressive approach when we are feeling resentful about something or feel something is unfair but don't have the leverage to change the situation. Baggage from the past typically comes in here where we want to make someone else suffer but aren't feeling brave enough to express our displeasure. The big problem with passive-aggressive communication is it is unclear and indirect; thus problems are rarely solved using this communication style, and this approach feeds resentment, anger, and dissatisfaction for both the recipient and the communicator.

CHAPTER 7:
SURVIVE STICKY SITUATIONS

TACTIC #59
OFTEN LIFE HAPPENS BECAUSE WE CREATED IT

THIS TIP ISN'T quite as quick as our other suggestions. It is a little more complex and, frankly, a lot more challenging to implement. However, it is critically important. And if you can get this, the rewards are dramatic.

Let me tell you a story to illustrate this important principle. A while back, I worked with juvenile delinquents enrolled in a program to help them turn their behavior around and (hopefully) become productive members of our society. One day, as I was coming into the probation building, I got into the elevator with one of the teens. He was wearing huge, baggy pants, a red t-shirt, a red hat, and red sneakers—clearly gang garb. He had a small "W" tattooed next to his eye (again a gang indicator, claiming "west side"). To top everything off, he was wearing a huge silver machine gun necklace on a conspicuous silver rope chain. A machine gun necklace. Seriously? When are you on your way to see your probation officer? This was not going to help him move forward in any way.

Now another kid I worked with at that same office came from a life much like the first guy. Both were young white men growing up in a terrible neighborhood with troubled backgrounds and similar awful disappointments from the grownups in their lives. This teen, however, had the foresight to recognize after he was arrested that he was at a crossroads. He could choose to continue down the path of multiple arrests and spend his life in and out of jail, or he could turn things around. He recommitted to high school, got a part-time job, quit the weed, dressed as best he could on minimum wage, and avoided (literally running from them at times) his gang member peers in his neighborhood. He got his attitude in check and figured out how to take responsibility for what he could change instead of just going along with what his neighborhood "expected" of him. He ended up on a full-ride scholarship to college. I still smile when I think of him.

Now while most of us reading this book haven't grown up in gang central and had to choose between continuing down a criminal path versus becoming a productive citizen, almost all of us have set ourselves up and been unpleasantly surprised by the results. I am *not* trying to blame the victim or encouraging self-loathing. Rather, I am trying to help us understand that our choices often lead us directly to where we are currently standing. This is fantastic news, because if we have contributed to our problems, then we can contribute to our solutions.

Thus, the tip here is for the long-term escape from sticky situations where you can't win. You can stop setting yourself up for failure and set yourself up for success instead. Start on the road to solution versus problem by looking at and truly examining your contribution to your current life. I bet you'll find you were there for at least some of it.

OFTEN LIFE HAPPENS BECAUSE WE CREATED IT WORKSHEET

Apply This: First, identify the things you are most unhappy about. What are your top five things that aren't going so well?

1.
2.
3.
4.
5.

Second, ask yourself how you have come to be in the middle of these unhappy circumstances. This is the tricky step because here, you need to move away from blaming others and life circumstances and, instead, take a close look at your own contributions to your life. Now obviously, there are some life events where we didn't have much of a contribution (blindsided in a car accident by a drunk driver), but we can take a close look at our *responses* to even these terrible, unhappy situations. For each of your top five above, write down your possible contribution to these situations.

1.
2.
3.
4.
5.

Third, identify your choices now to move toward a better circumstance. What can you do today, tomorrow, next week, or over the next year to dig yourself out of the hole you walked, fell, or dove into? After all, no matter how the hole got there, it's still a hole. And if you're going to feel better, you're going to have to start climbing out.

1.
2.
3.
4.
5.

Here's an example. Are you stuck in a dead-end job with a lousy boss? Okay, time to examine what choices you made to stay in this job. This is *not* the bit about how circumstances, your parents, mean people, etc., *made* you take this position. Look at how you are participating in the problem. Now, see what your options are to improve your future. Maybe you can improve your attitude at this job, or maybe you can brush up on your resume and apply to other places, but no matter what, you do *not* have to stay stuck. The choice to remain in a bad situation is one kind of response. The choice to get moving in a different direction is another.

TACTIC #60
DRAW STRAWS

ONE OF THE weirdest, most agonizing feelings in life is that of getting stuck, truly horribly stuck, frozen in time, trying to make a difficult choice. Hopefully, you are stuck between a couple of great options rather than a rock and a hard place, but nonetheless, it is incredibly frustrating to feel like you just don't know how to choose or that any choice is somehow fraught with peril.

A delightful young woman I worked with came in to see me, stuck on how to choose between colleges. The deadline for her to accept was coming up fast, and she still had no idea which school was the best choice for her, despite weeks of trying to figure it out. She agonized so much about this choice that she was having trouble getting her homework done and felt sick to her stomach.

We went through the pros and cons of each college, ran numbers for which would make more financial sense, identified the family, peer, or support factors present in each choice, and tried to figure out which college had more intrinsic gut-level appeal. All to no avail. She kept getting the same answers she had gotten on her own, with one place a clearly better financial decision, another more appealing because it was closer to home, but both providing a solid education and good social opportunities. Her family saw the same pros and cons and, as a result, were fully supportive of either choice.

I decided to provide her with a challenge. I had her draw straws, with the instruction that she would choose the college that came out in the contest. (I wouldn't have held her to the choice; that, of course, was for her and her parents to decide.) I cut out two pieces of paper and put the name of each college on the end in my hand, scrambled them, and had her choose. What happened? Well, she drew the name of a college and immediately reacted, totally bummed. She knew at that moment that she wanted to go to the other college.

APPLY THIS: Here's the thing: on a gut level, we often know the correct choice instinctively. But we get hung up intellectually, on the pros or the cons, on the "shoulds" or the "supposed to's." We start trying to predict the future instead of making the best choice we can in the moment with the information we have in front of us.

Take a decision you are immobilized about. Create "straws" and scramble them. Take a few deep breaths and ask your wisest self to help you think about this choice. Then draw straws and see what your reaction is. Totally psyched? Could be the choice for you. Super disappointed? Maybe you are clearer than you thought. This activity helps you tune in better to your inner knowledge and helps you listen to yourself more clearly.

TACTIC #61

WHY NOT ASK?

At the tender age of nineteen, I received some of the best advice in the world from my fabulous dad. Once we talked about it, I couldn't believe he had waited so long to give it to me.

What advice, you ask? Well, the advice was three simple words: "Why not ask?" His advice, relevant to some quandary incredibly important at the time, but nothing I can remember now, was to simply *ask* for what I wanted. "Why not ask?" he said. And *bam. Pow*—my world opened before my very eyes.

Why *not* ask? Maybe you won't get the answer you want; maybe someone will tell you no; maybe he or she will be rude or dismissive in their denial. People can be like that sometimes. But sometimes, they are surprisingly happy to oblige. Maybe, just maybe, you will get exactly what you are looking for. Ever since then, now over thirty years later, I have been implementing those three little words with terrific success.

Now, those things I would normally assume are impossible, I ask for. I use this too when I am confused and need clarification, if I'm feeling dumb or clueless, or if I am just super curious about something. Do I always get what I am looking for? Absolutely not, but there have been several instances where the *act of asking* has changed a situation entirely. This works just as well with the big stuff (promotion, raise, date with that person you've had your eyes on forever) and the little stuff (flight upgrade, help out of a late fee). Also, it can be helpful with interpersonal stuff. I have asked why certain policies are in place, what someone's intentions are, if I can help someone in need, and if I can beg out of an obligation—you get the picture.

Now, one of the tricks to this nifty little technique is that you have to ask without entitlement, with no assumption that you *deserve* what you are asking for. The act of asking is simply a question, not an expectation of an answer. So, once you have asked, it is generally best to accept the answer rather than chafe against it. Of course, some things aren't appropriate to ask for or ask about, but I leave it to your good judgment to determine when it is best to leave something unrequested. Overall, however, I encourage you to try it out and (hopefully) enjoy the outcome.

APPLY THIS: The next time you are feeling stymied and uncertain, why not ask? Really wanting a particular outcome but afraid to ask for it? Ask. Curious about something but don't want to look stupid? Take the risk and ask. Make sure to ask without expectation and to ask with humility, but ask away. I bet you'll like the results. People often *do* want to help, if they can, but they'll never get the chance if they don't know what you want. And if you're worried about offending somebody, this is a great chance to reframe. It's more considerate to give them the chance to respond to your true desire rather than expecting everybody to be psychic all the time. So, ask and see what happens.

TACTIC #62
HONOR YOUR BEST SELF

ONE OF THE oldest, most frequently utilized, and easiest psychological tests to give someone is what is called a "Mental Status Examination." Tons of folks, from first responder EMTs to doctors to psychologists, will give some variety of this test. Basically, it asks questions that are easy to answer if you are in your right mind.

Some of the Mental Status Exams are quite quick (do you know your name, date, surroundings?), while some are much more detailed and extensive. Most, especially the more detailed ones, involve asking folks about their ability to apply reasoning and judgment. It is fascinating when people *know* the right answer but tell me they would make the wrong choice under certain circumstances. It is even more fascinating to watch people know the right answer and repeatedly make the wrong choice. What's happening in these situations is that people are not acting from their best selves. Rather they are rationalizing why breaking the rules (and doing what they know to be wrong) is okay.

Here are some examples. Have a stinky banana peel in your car but no trash can in sight? You know the right thing to do is to wait until you find a trash can, but you throw the banana peel out the window anyway because you rationalize your way into the wrong answer. "Oh, it's okay; it's natural. It will decompose; nobody will notice." Or that sweater that fell apart after you washed it, even though the label said to dry clean it? You know it isn't quite right to return it because you didn't follow the instructions, but you manage to convince yourself it's fine. You may even lie to the salesperson, saying that you followed the directions when you know you didn't. Totally broke? Find a wallet in a store and no one is around? You know the right thing is to return it, but you rifle through and keep the cash. It's fair to say these actions don't come from your best self. No matter how broke you are, it isn't right to fix that problem with someone else's cash. Ever.

APPLY THIS: The next time you find yourself in a sticky (or smelly, as in the banana peel example) situation, act from your best self. Think about what you would want to teach a child in the situation. I bet you wouldn't want to teach them to litter, lie, or steal, so hold yourself to that standard. Check-in with the part of your stomach that twists a little when you know you're doing something wrong. Ignore the rationalizing thoughts: *Just this once*, *No one will see me*, *It isn't a big deal*, or *I can get away with it*. Choose the right path—the one that honors your best self, the one that you would be proud to be seen doing and be pleased to model for others. I promise it will make you feel much better, both in the short and long term.

TACTIC #63
YOU ARE WHO YOU HANG OUT WITH

There is this silly, funny '90s Adam Sandler movie called *Billy Madison*, where Sandler plays the role of an overindulged twenty-something who gets challenged to make something of himself.[12] He drinks all day with his going-nowhere friends, takes advantage of his dad's good faith and money, and assumes success will be handed to him despite his absurd behavior. But he's unhappy and hates being considered a joke in his family, so he decides to improve himself. He starts working hard, studying, cleaning up his appearance, improving his behavior, and demands that his friends change along with him. In the end (of course), he gets the girl, wins the contest, and earns his father's approval. Now life is certainly no Adam Sandler movie, but the basic premise is correct: you are, to a huge degree, who you hang out with.

In fact, you can generally tell an enormous amount about someone's life by looking at how, where, and with whom they are choosing to spend their time. Smoking pot all day with your friends? Chances are, you are a lot less motivated and less successful than the person who isn't abusing drugs. Now, if smoking pot all day is what you want, fine. However, if you want to be more successful, you might need to rethink your choices, including choices about how you spend your time and who you spend that time with. Now before you start complaining that I sound just like your mom, telling you not to hang out with Billy down the street because he's up to no good, pause for a second. Was your mom right? Was Billy up to no good? Most likely. And, the even bigger question, where, oh where, is good ole Billy now?

The power of your immediate peers can be seen in this Law of Five; your weight, salary, number of children, number of drinks per night, even how often you attend church—all of these things can be reliably predicted by averaging yourself with your closest five friends. It is scary how closely these numbers line up. The power of association should not be underestimated.

THINK ABOUT THIS: Who are you associating with? Are they going places? Making good choices? Taking care of themselves? Do they bathe? Do you? It may behoove you to start challenging yourself to widen your circle and to begin associating more with folks who share your goals or have already succeeded in certain aspects of their lives. It doesn't matter if you are a teenager or an adult, social worker, or CEO; this isn't about status; this is about surrounding yourself with excellence. Hang out less with the folks who are dragging you down and hang out more with folks who lift you up. Challenge yourself to move to the next level in functioning and be with people who represent more of what you want to see in your life.

TACTIC #64
SINGLE-TASKING

When was the last time you left the house without your cell phone? Do you find yourself making dinner but also watching the TV on the counter and catching up with your kids at the same time? Watering your lawn while thinking about that report due on Monday at work? We are constantly, overwhelmingly, relentlessly, a multitasking society. We have convinced ourselves (erroneously, I might add) that we are most efficient when we are attending to more than one thing at a time. We are constantly being interrupted and most often trying to cram two, three, or even more things into one time period. We have created an entire culture of distraction, which is leaving us with partial and mediocre completion on many tasks, creating a cycle of inefficiency and feeling overwhelmed.

There is some interesting information about interruptions, suggesting that for every interruption, it takes us between fifteen to twenty minutes to recover our full attention to the task we were focusing on. Can you imagine, then, the impact of being interrupted every couple of minutes? Do we *ever* get to focus on anything? Not so much.

Here is a suggestion. Instead of constantly multitasking, try switching your attention to consistent "single-tasking." Focus on one item at a time for an allotted amount of time. This builds a habit of concentration and takes you into a new realm of productivity. Schedule times to attend to tasks and try to focus on one task at a time, as much as possible. It is amazing how much more efficiently we can accomplish things when we are not constantly torn in multiple directions. The benefits of single-tasking are vast, but, most importantly, things tend to take less time when you are single-tasking than when you are trying to get many things done at once.

APPLY THIS: Here are some ideas for implementation in a variety of environments: At work, instead of letting email and phone calls interrupt your day all day, try setting aside time to focus on your task list without interruption. Have designated times during the day when you take a break for email, entertain interruptions by co-workers, and respond to phone calls. Leave a message on your phone and email about the times you respond, and vigorously protect that focused time. Then, once home, separate your work and home life. Try to leave work at work or allot specific times at home you spend time on work items. Spend one-on-one time, without interruption, with your children, your friends, your partner. Have systems in place to complete household tasks and focus on just that one task while completing it. Have times set aside for meals, recreation, and exercise, and then take them individually, one at a time. Commit to single-tasking as much as you can. The benefits are staggering.

TACTIC #65

APOLOGIES AND FORGIVENESS—WHEN YOU'VE REALLY SCREWED UP

One of the lousiest experiences in life is when we have done something wrong. Maybe we've hurt someone's feelings, destroyed trust, or interfered in business that wasn't ours to mess with. Maybe we behaved in a way that got us into trouble. After the dust has settled, we will usually want forgiveness from others when we have done something wrong. How do we properly apologize? Should we ask for forgiveness? Do we deserve to be forgiven? Our desire to feel better about what we have done, and to know the wronged person can feel better too, are typical, regardless of the nature of the offense.

What exactly constitutes a positive apology? How do you earn the forgiveness of the wronged party? First, you must stop thinking about yourself. Thinking about yourself, incidentally, is probably what got you into this mess in the first place. You need to move beyond your desire to escape from guilt and your expectation that the wronged person is somehow obligated to forgive you. In short, take responsibility and view the issue from the wronged person's point of view, instead of through your self-centered eyes. Second, focus on making amends for your wrong. Finally, it is critically important to relinquish your desire for reconciliation and instead accept that, sometimes, your attempts at restitution may not be met with a restored relationship.

HERE IS WHAT THIS LOOKS LIKE IN ACTION:

A while back, I was talking to a friend of mine. As moms do, we were talking about our kids. I ended up sharing something that my daughter had confided in me about and, frankly, I didn't think much more about it. I figured this was what moms do. We occasionally commiserate about parenting and share the trials and tribulations of our kids' experiences. What I did not pay attention to, however, was how my daughter would feel when it came to her attention that I had shared this information. Spoiler alert: She was mad. Really mad. She felt I had violated her confidence and was especially angry since I hold secrets all the time as a standard practice in my work but didn't consider keeping her stuff private. Big mistake on my part.

Wow, I needed to apologize. It went a little like this: "I am so, so sorry that I shared that information without considering what you would want. Please let me know if there is anything I can do to make it up to you. Moving forward, I will check with you first before sharing our conversations, even with friends."

Now, you may be thinking, "Okay, Dr. Carrie, but the thing I did is a lot, lot worse than your temporary failure to be sensitive and considerate." Fair enough. I, too, have done worse things than this, but the ingredients of a quality apology remain the same. Avoid, too, what my friend Ellen calls the "explain-ology," where you spend your valuable apology time explaining why you did this crappy thing. This is tantamount to justification.

Don't justify. Accept responsibility, apologize from the heart, and figure out how to make amends. Reach out, apologize, and ask for forgiveness.

TACTIC #66
THE CUPCAKE METHOD OF RECOVERY

There is a terrific children's book by Judith Viorst called *Alexander and the Terrible, Horrible, No Good, Very Bad Day* that I was thinking about a while back, after having a terrible, horrible, no good, ridiculously bad day of my own.[13] Really, in many ways, it was a bad day at the end of a bad month (tax issues, health issues, car accident, business stress, travel problems), which made the bad day feel really, really bad. I felt awful. However, I am supposed to be an expert in behavior, a positive psychology advocate, and a resilient person. Most of the time, I can live up to my roles as a good psychologist and a good person and attempt to be a calm, reasonable role model who handles stress well. But even those of us who preach and practice this stuff all day long can be pushed to our limits.

What did I do? I called "Uncle" and admitted I was in over my head. I took some deep breaths and acknowledged my complex, cranky emotions. I called a supportive friend and then a supportive family member and admitted I was struggling and feeling hopeless and overwhelmed. It took both phone calls to be reminded about the good stuff in my life. Then I abandoned the humungous list of chores I was planning to do. I gathered up my kiddo, and we went to get cupcakes and milk. We sat outside and munched on cupcakes, and let go of all the rest. The returns didn't get made to the store; no dice on the fancy Sunday dinner. The laundry didn't get done either. In fact, nothing much got done at all.

But what did happen was that I was able to settle down, enjoy being with my child, and let all the stress go for a little bit. Cupcakes, it seems, can solve big problems sometimes. Now, notice that I didn't go on a binge (just one cupcake, thanks), I didn't go out and start acting in horribly self-sabotaging ways (just say no to the triple scotch or the slot machines), I didn't rail my frustrations at others. Rather, I took a moment to treat myself to some (delicious) downtime. I picked myself up and dusted myself off the next day, started in on the chores, planned to deal with the problems, and returned to my regular routine, all in about twenty-four hours.

APPLY THIS: The next time you have the worst day ever, and your usual tricks aren't working you may want to try giving up the fight and settle instead for some downtime. Get a little support and then do something different to move away from all that stress. Take a break, recharge, and then reassess your situation. Maybe your "cupcake" isn't a cupcake at all. It could be a long run, tea with a friend, journaling a dramatic dialogue of the conversation you wish you could have, or playing at the dog park with your favorite four-legged friend. Whatever it is, indulge for a bit and let that recharge give you the energy to move away from your horrible day and create a better one tomorrow. As you know, it's only a day away.

TACTIC #67
BE ANTI-ALLIGATOR
*A GOING DEEPER TIP

That wrinkly, curly gray mess we call our brain is not just one big blob. In fact, we can roughly divide our brains into our reptile (primitive) brain, our mammalian (emotional) brain, and our human (logical) brain. These three parts each have valuable functions, but when they are not communicating well, or when the wrong part of your brain is responding to a situation, things can get messy. And confusing.

The reptile brain makes up the base of our brain and controls things such as breathing and our flight-or-fight mechanism. Our mammal brain is our central station, so to speak, and houses our emotional centers. Our human brain is the machine in the front and houses our logical, rational, and reasoning centers, along with our ability to perform metacognition, the ability to *think* about our thinking. (Like this: *I think I'll make steak when the Smiths come over. Oh, what a silly thought, they're vegetarians.*)

Ever hung out with an alligator? They will respond behaviorally for food, shelter, or danger, but they are not what you'd call bonders. They are instinctually driven creatures reacting in simple, predictable ways to situations. Now, if you've spent much time with mammals, you know they have a wide range of emotional responses, establish clear preferences in attachments, and can communicate with some precision about their feelings. Ask just about any mammal lover, and they can tell you a story about their animal feeling something strongly and acting accordingly. For example, the dog feeling super excited about taking a walk, the horse who played tag with a child (seriously, I've seen it with my own eyes), and the cat who would get visibly sad when she saw the luggage being taken out. For the human brain, we use higher-level rational and reasoning skills, analyze incoming information, and adjust reactions accordingly.

Knowing about our brains can help us understand more about our reactions to situations and help our human, logical brain call the shots more often. Ever heard a loud noise behind you and found yourself turning around to see what it was without thinking? Of course, you have. That is your most basic brain functioning; from your fight-or-flight mechanism, you are checking to see if there is danger. Now, imagine a time when you have felt emotionally overwhelmed, either with positive or negative emotion, and you couldn't think of how or what to say but could feel the strength of your emotion. That's your mammal brain working. Now, in both cases, it helps to give yourself a moment to process the experiences and then make choices about how to respond. Think there's danger? Your body will react first, but then you can assess the situation and respond. Emotionally overwrought? Give yourself enough time and space to evaluate, consider, and choose a response based on assessment instead of emotional reactivity.

APPLY THIS: Next time you are in a sticky situation, check in with yourself to see where you are responding from in your brain. Challenge yourself to involve your higher-order thinking and processing skills instead of reacting from your snappy alligator or your luggage-threatened cat.

TACTIC #68
HABIT = DESTINY
*A GOING DEEPER TIP

Most of what we do each day falls into the category of habit. We generally have a mixture of helpful habits and not so helpful ones, and most of us repeat our habits over and over again (hence, you see, the meaning of the word). We tend to have habits that function logically, physically, behaviorally, interpersonally, and emotionally. Quick, what do you think about your mother-in-law? How long have you thought this? Do you love broccoli or hate it? How many times a week do you exercise? Where do you fill up your car with gas? If you are like most people, even if you aren't a fit-the-mold kind of person, you answered those questions with habitual opinions, thoughts, emotions, and behaviors. I would also guess that you weren't aware of how many things you do that are governed by habit.

How we approach life determines our habits, and our habits, in turn, determine our approach. And thus, the habits we implement on a regular basis, both positive and negative, create who we are. After all, we are what we do every day. Now, are you ready for the beautiful power in this realization? Most of us have a ho-hum reaction to the habitual, but once we recognize that we can change our habits, we can change our destiny. For reals.

See a person who is super fit? I bet he has habits (hopefully good, healthy ones) that create that level of fitness. See a person who is successful at work? I bet she has habits leading her toward that success.

Chapter 7: Survive Sticky Situations

APPLY THIS: Examine your habits. Besides the obvious, like how many times a day you brush your teeth, look at the more complex "habits" you hold dear. Are you a reactive person in conflict? Is this helping you? Maybe you need a new habit to breathe first, take ten minutes, and then respond to heated situations. Are you a person who is constantly getting taken advantage of by others? Maybe you have a habit of saying yes when you mean no, or maybe you have a habit of letting folks talk down to you. Take a peek at the habits you repeat daily and honestly appraise if they are helping you move forward or holding you back from success. Then implement some changes to create new habits.

Creating new habits can feel like a ton of work. Changing habits is best done from a place of true conviction, supported by behavioral shifts. For just about any unhelpful habit you want to shift to a skillful one, it is helpful to first align this new habit with your core values, then identify the small, medium, and large behavior shifts you need to implement to make it happen. Practice your new habit for at least twenty-one days, and then reassess. Ignore and resist impulses to go back to your old, negative habit, and challenge yourself to implement the new behaviors regularly. If you slip up, resist the temptation to waste valuable time beating yourself up. Just draw a line and get right back to your new behavior *ASAP*.

PART III:

MOVE FORWARD

IMPLEMENTING CHANGE CAN be seriously difficult. Our brains are hardwired to be as "efficient" as possible, and our brain's idea of efficiency is a bit, well, strange. Efficiency to our brains is linked to survival, so something is considered "efficient" and, thus, worth replicating if it didn't kill you the last time you did it. This is why things like commercials that encourage you to stop smoking because "it will hurt you down the road" don't work all that well. Dying (admittedly a horrible, painful death) from emphysema in sixty years doesn't make your brain motivated to change today.

Another major problem with changing, doing things differently, or moving forward is that our brains are naturally set up to resist change. In fact, our brains are so good at being "efficient" that they tell us *not* to change sometimes, even when a change would do us good. Ever tried to change something? It tends to feel uncomfortable, right?

Let's take an example less complex than quitting smoking (which involves both a mental and a physiological component to the addiction). How about even just changing the way you brush your teeth? I am assuming here that you have two operational hands, but you most likely use one of them to brush your teeth every morning. If you try using your non-dominant hand, it feels strange. Pretty soon, your brain will start telling you, "this isn't working," or "this is silly," or "this is too hard," and you will switch back to your dominant hand. This pattern can be expected with just about any change you are trying to make; your brain wants you to do things the same way, the "efficient" way. Not so efficient, huh?

How do we work around all this old hardwiring? Well, we help our brains by changing slowly and doing it in ways that build on habit patterns that are already working well. We increase awareness of what makes us stuck, stressed, and unhappy, and then make a good solid plan about how to implement some new habits. We become flexible in the face of problems. Try new habits to replace the ones that might be "efficient" to our brains but are not efficient in our lives at all. You can alter those old unhelpful habits and make new patterns that truly are efficient.

This section of the book gives you all sorts of information about how to battle the "efficiency" issue more effectively in our brains. We discuss how to move forward in your relationships, how to get clever about avoiding stress when you can and managing it when it is unavoidable, and, finally, we'll cover some lovely information on how to make your life as close to the ideal version you dream about.

CHAPTER 8:
ENHANCE RELATIONSHIPS

TACTIC #69
IDEAL OTHER EXERCISE

Dating? We all want a perfect fit. However, since perfect is not available (life is more interesting than that), let's help you get to an ideal match for you. This is one of my favorite exercises in therapy. Start with a blank piece of paper and write out a list of qualities, values, and characteristics that, all put together, sound like an ideal mate. There are four corners to the work: shallow, deep, generic, and unique. All four corners are important and should be represented in about equal amounts. Make sure to address the top five categories of potential arguments (more on this later in this chapter). Finally, review the whole list and see what the truly non-negotiable things are, then put a little star by them. (Remember, you are *not* going to get every single attribute on this list. You are hoping for about 80–90 percent of the list, with 100 percent of the non-negotiables represented.)

HERE GOES: MY IDEAL (MAN, WOMAN):

Shallow: These are the surface things like height, weight, eye and hair color, and fashion sense.

Deep: These are the important shared values, religious beliefs, family style, and life goals.

Generic: The not exciting characteristics, but important to you, such as job type, education level, and interest in fitness.

Unique: These are the special qualities you truly desire to complement your lifestyle. Love to camp? Your ideal needs to go with you. Can't cook? Your ideal will. You get the idea.

Now onto those top five categories so you can avoid arguments by being on the same page:

Sex: What attributes suggest sexual compatibility?

Money: How do you want your ideal mate to manage their funds? Credit? Retirement?

Family/Social: Hoping for someone close to their family? Tons of friends or a few?

Parenting: What parenting style are you hoping for? Desired number of kids to have?

Religion/Values: What values, principles, and spiritual beliefs are important to you?

I typically advise folks that they put down a few "givens," things they should just expect to be true, the absence of which guarantees acres of avoidable misery. Some of those givens are things like no active addictions, fight fair, no abuse, no cruelty to animals, etc.

Make up your list and see the picture of your ideal mate emerge. Make sure to look through and pick those things you can't live without and those you could compromise on. Then examine your dating prospects with these criteria at hand and see how they match up.

IDEAL OTHER EXERCISE WORKSHEET

Give yourself a few minutes to fill this out. Then show it to your loved ones so they can help you see what you might be missing. Hang it on your fridge and look at it after each date. If your date doesn't measure up to around the 80–90 percent level, move on to a different person.

Chapter 8: Enhance Relationships

Shallow	Deep
Generic	Unique
Sex	Money
Family/Social	Kids/Parenting
Religion/Values	Givens

TACTIC #70
THE THREE-LEGGED STOOL OF RELATIONSHIPS

A DEAR OLDER WOMAN I had the privilege of knowing used to make furniture. She would paint these intricate patterns and flowers in an old Dutch tradition. Her strongest piece was a three-legged stool; it could hold over three hundred pounds. However, if the legs weren't properly in place, the whole thing would dump you on your butt. Relationships, I decided a while back, are like that three-legged stool. If you have the three building blocks firmly in place, not much is stronger. But trying to balance on one or two legs is disastrous.

Here are the three legs of the relationship stool:

1. Attraction
2. Fit
3. Timing

Attraction refers to all those lovely feelings where you want to move closer, snuggle up, canoodle, spend time together, gaze at the person across the room, feel that special something when you see them, want to get them home and rip off all their clothes. You know: Attraction, desire, and passion. This is the most instinctual leg, meaning chemistry is typically either on or off and doesn't usually grow much over time. This is important to remember when you find yourself feeling guilty that you don't feel that spark for that kind, successful person who looks great on paper.

Fit refers to lots of things you probably wrote down on your ideal person list. This is the most internal, personal leg. Fit consists of the shared values, similar and complementary goals for life, shared desires and hopes for the future, commonalities, and interests that match up. Fit is the glue that keeps things together even if one of the other legs wobbles a bit over time (while fixing that wobble is super important, fit can carry you through for a while). Fit is the fun stuff that keeps you *friends* with your ideal person over the long term. Fit is comfortable, enjoyable, interesting, and fun.

Timing is all those external things that can get in the way of a relationship being successful. Timing is why most high school sweethearts don't make it because they find each other too early. Similarly, timing is why long-distance relationships are so hard; the distance isn't the right length at the right time. Timing means that both people will be ready for a relationship, both single and interested in dating, both at the same developmental stage in life (this explains why those relationships with a twenty-year age difference tend to get hard over time). Timing means it is right, *right now*, to pursue each other.

APPLY THIS: Put attraction, fit, and timing together, and boy, do you have a solid combo. Missing a leg? See if you can make a fix; if not, he/she is not likely the right person for the long haul. Trying to get by with only one leg? Time to move on and find a more complete relationship. You deserve the whole package, and that complete package helps keep things steady and healthy in a long-term relationship.

TACTIC #71
REPLACEMENT PARTS WILL ALWAYS BE ON BACKORDER—ALWAYS

One of the things I am asked for most often in my therapy practice is to help folks navigate romantic relationships. People want to get in them, they want to get out of them, and they want to meet and marry "The One." They are often waiting around, hoping for the exact right person to suddenly appear in their life. Or they are in a relationship and are disappointed when their partner isn't perfect. I hate to be the bearer of bad news, but the thing is, no one is perfect. No one. Nobody, not even that hot guy on the second floor who looks so incredible and smells delicious when you pass in the hall. Not even that gal your mom really likes.

What is a person to do when their (imperfect) significant other is driving them crazy? Well, imagine placing an order for replacement parts and then imagine that the order is on indefinite backorder. Now, this technique works best when you have chosen a good fit for a mate in the first place and are putting in the work on your relationship to keep it fresh, supportive, and loving. This way, you will always have a small order of "parts" you'd love to replace, but you aren't looking to place an order for a completely new model. This notion of a backorder allows you to place your attention on the working parts.

Here are some examples of "parts" to put on backorder and just let them be. Nothing to try to scramble and fix, just things you wish your partner would do/be/have that you can set aside so you can focus on all the good things in your relationship:

- Your guy won't go to the opera with you? Neither will mine. I go with my friends.
- Your gal won't hunt with you? Neither will I. Please, go with your friends.
- Wish your person were more social? Okay, negotiate for important events; let go of the rest.
- Your spouse not much of a political pundit? No worries, enjoy your daily dose online and talk about it with your buddy down the hall at work who loves that stuff.
- Are you a morning person, but your mate isn't? Make time for each other when it works for both of you. Compromise on bedtime and waking times.

APPLY THIS: Let go of that little stuff by imagining a "backorder" list that is never going to be filled. Figure out workarounds and enjoy "your" things on your own time, and let your significant other enjoy his/her interests as well. Respect each other's basic natures. Stop trying to make your partner think or behave exactly as you do. Let go and let yourself enjoy what does work, where you both do line up, and the things that make your relationship sizzle. The mystery of another human being is a continuous wonder that can keep you curious for years, so long as you're not too busy finding fault with their inability to put the toilet paper on the roll in the right direction.

Bonus tip: This works well with your friends, family members, and co-workers too. Try it out.

TACTIC #72
THE IDEAL POSITIVE TO NEGATIVE RATIO

IMAGINE THE FOLLOWING scenario with me: You wake up, have a nice breakfast, and take the dog for a walk. It's sunny outside and just the right temperature. You go to the local park and smile at the other nice people walking their dogs. You even get to see a puppy or two. The walk is pleasant and not rushed, comfortable and enjoyable. Suddenly, a big aggressive dog lunges at your dog, almost nipping your sweet baby. You get your dog and yourself out of the way just in time, even though the aggressive dog's owner is no help and even a little rude about it all. "Hey, dogs will be dogs."

Later in your day, what do you remember? I promise the most predominant memory of the morning won't be the pile of positives; it will be that awful big dog and his terrible owner. Why? This is an old survival mechanism hardwired into our brains. We are much, much more likely to track, remember, detail, and *feel* negatives. There is an adage in the neuropsychology world that is true: our brains are like Teflon (think super slippery) for positives and Velcro (think super sticky) for negatives. While this is a fabulous way to keep ourselves alive in a threatening world, it doesn't do much for our moods and is especially troublesome in relationships.

Overall, you can count on negatives being heard more loudly and kept in memory much longer than positives. We can often count the number of insults but barely remember a single compliment. There are a variety of studies out there asserting the various positive to negative ratios we need, ranging from two positives to every negative to up to nine positives for every negative. I typically split the difference and teach clients that we need about five positive experiences to every negative, at the same level of emotional intensity, to keep our heads securely out of the oven.

That little caveat at the end about being *at the same level of emotional intensity* is especially important. This is why you can do nice things all day for someone, have a lovely time together, trade delightful compliments, and still lose all of it when you're tired later and snap about something not being right. The snap plays louder than all the nice stuff because the emotional intensity of a mean-spirited comment is bigger than the emotional intensity of the basic niceties.

APPLY THIS: Notice your ratio of positives to negatives in your interactions. Be thoughtful with critical feedback, and be careful your delivery isn't so harsh that it is going to wash away all your positive interactions. Make sure you are trying hard to compliment more than you criticize. Give credit for what is working, remind people when they are doing things right, notice the good stuff. Highlight what *is* working. You can use this in your romantic relationships, with friendships and family members, and even with yourself. Maybe you've felt ashamed that you get so gobsmacked by one nasty negative that you forget the good. But you can let go of that because it's not a character flaw. It's biology.

TACTIC #73

FIX THE TOP FIVE CATEGORIES OF ARGUMENT

Gotten into an argument with your significant other recently? I bet it was about one of the top five things most couples fight about: sex, money, family, values, or children/parenting. Seriously, think about an argument you have had recently; it had something to do with these categories, didn't it?

One person messy and the other neat? Values argument. One person wants sex three times a day and another three times a year? Obviously, an argument regarding intimacy issues. Arguing about the in-laws? Ah, family. At odds about how to discipline your kids? Parenting argument. And then there is the big daddy of the argument pentagon, the one that seems to happen every month when you are paying your bills: the financial argument.

What is a person to do? Well, your first step is getting clear about the typical category of argument in your household. Is there one that is a frequent hot button? Maybe a combination of categories gets you and your partner in trouble? Hopefully, you aren't fighting in all five categories at once. If so, you *may* want to go back and review the "Ideal Other" tip #69. (No, seriously, that's what number it is.)

After you have gotten clear on the category of your favorite argument, it is worth your time to examine the typical triggers that rev up that conflict. Once you are aware of both the category (or categories) and the triggers, then you have some real options for change. That awareness gives you the clues to discovering a solution, so you can have a conversation about the *category* instead of an argument about the special sauce of the details of this fight on this day.

APPLY THIS: First, start by identifying your typical category of argument. Is it sex, money, family, values, or kids? Then, sit down with your partner (when you are both calm) and discuss the category. Resist the urge to have the same argument and talk instead about how to fix the category conflict.

Let's look at an example. One person a mess, one person neat? One person doesn't fuss about having everything in the right place; the other feels out of control and crazy when things are out of place. This is a great recipe for an ongoing, frustrating impasse, an argument that continues over time without a solution. Now the task is to take the messy-neat dichotomy and to start talking about a compromise. Maybe messy-neat can become messy in the garage but neat in the kitchen; maybe you figure out an organizational system that works for you both (a drawer without much structure for the messy, a file cabinet with dedicated files for the neat). You get the picture. Discuss the category, look for the triggers, identify solutions and talk about how to meet in the middle. Then try out the solution and see if it softens the issue.

SELF-HELP ON THE GO

TACTIC #74
RECOGNIZE DIFFERENT LOVE LANGUAGES

ONCE UPON A time, there was an incredible snowstorm in Denver. Denver is a high desert, and huge, city-burying snowstorms don't happen all that often. This one, however, was a doozy, and close to two feet of snow fell in about twelve hours overnight. A young lady spent the night at a friend's house downtown that night, wisely not taking her low-clearance car through the storm. The next day, now stranded in said low clearance car, she called her boyfriend, who (naturally) drove a four-wheel-drive vehicle. He came all the way down and shoveled out her car. Then, he drove her car home while she followed in his high clearance 4x4. Later, snug back at her place, the young lady brought up an issue she had meant to talk to her boyfriend about for a while. The issue, you ask? Well, she told him that she needed him to be clearer about his feelings and to tell her how he felt about her. To which the boyfriend replied, "I just did."

This is an awesome example of a difference in love languages. Did the girlfriend appreciate the gesture of the rescue and ride home? Absolutely. But was she paying attention to what this meant from the boyfriend? Definitely not. She thought he was being nice and was waiting for *words* to know he loved her. What did the boyfriend think? Well, he thought his *actions* translated into "I love you. Lots."

Most of us have one or more "love languages." A language (big surprise) can be verbal, like saying "I love you." But it can also be expressed through actions (coming home to a clean house pretty much says "I love you" to me in a major way), by spending quality time with each other, by giving gifts, through physical touch. It can be expressed through sweet gestures, writing letters, holding hands, or helping someone move their grandparents. The idea here is that different people express love differently. Similarly, different people receive love differently. What may be a huge expression of love to one (driving in a snowstorm for a rescue) may be received as something nice but not be understood or received as *love*.

APPLY THIS: The trick is to become an expert, both at identifying what your preferred love language is and then becoming an expert about your significant other's love language. Think about what makes a difference to you. What lifts your heart, makes you smile, helps you feel loved? How about your partner? If you aren't sure, you can observe them, notice what makes a difference. Or ask. The goal here isn't to judge someone's love language as wrong because it is different than yours. Rather it is to honor their language while asking for love to be given to you in yours. This lets everybody off the hook and gives us one more glorious opportunity to appreciate that *other people are not exactly like us*. Which is why we are sleeping with them. Check out the book that introduced this concept, *The Five Love Languages* by Gary Chapman, to get more info on this topic.[14] And remember, this same stuff works with friends, children, co-workers, and family, not just your romantic partner.

TACTIC #75

WANT TO AVOID A RELATIONSHIP CATASTROPHE? BEWARE OF CRITICISM, CONTEMPT, AND OTHER HARSH RESPONSES

I MUST ADMIT I am a bit of a voyeur. I am constantly on the lookout for people behaving in ways that bring them closer to others, helps their relationships flourish, and makes them feel good. I am always thrilled to see the magical dance of a happy couple. I notice when my friend's husband brings her flowers (a favorite treat she'll never buy for herself), or when my friend makes dinner for her husband because she knows he's had a hell of a day. How fun it is to hear couples compliment each other, or to see people in a thirty-year marriage hold hands on the beach. In short, I'm watching real life prove what couples researchers have been telling us for years: happy couples relate like good friends, handle disagreements in calm, gentle ways, and make repairs to their relationship as needed.

Those who remain unhappily married and those who divorce tend to have a high level of negative interaction and go to harsh, destructive, distancing behaviors, especially when they fight. The four worst offenders, according to famous couples researchers, John and Julie Gottman? Well, those would be criticism, contempt, defensiveness, and stonewalling.[15] All of these responses distance you from the person you are talking to be it your partner, spouse, child, friend, colleague—pretty much anyone. Imagine that. People don't like to be treated like crap.

When you criticize, you tend to make a sweeping generalization about what is wrong with your partner. You might say they are selfish, unkind, bad in bed, sloppy, etc. Contempt takes criticism to the next level by putting the other person down while elevating yourself. Something like, "I know what I'm talking about. You're an idiot." And then there's the lovely play of defensiveness, often paired with criticism and contempt, sometimes happening all by its glorious self. This is when we protect ourselves against attack by defending our position, without considering how both parties (even perfectly innocent us) might have an impact on a situation. We take zero responsibility for our part, wanting only to blame the other person. Finally, there is stonewalling, where you emotionally distance from relating. We roll our eyes in conversation or look away, refusing to acknowledge our partner's obviously irrelevant point of view.

TRY THIS INSTEAD: Replace criticism, contempt, defensiveness, and stonewalling with healthier behaviors. Overall, you want to strive to notice the good in your partner, not just the bad. It is important to try to imagine yourself on the same level, not putting anyone down in conversation. Try to value your significant other, even when you are angry. This means listening (really listening, not waiting for your mate to stop talking) and trying to figure out your part in a conflict. Finally, it means engaging instead of withdrawing in conversations, even the hard ones. This doesn't mean that you should pretend your partner (friend, boss, colleague, etc.) is perfect and does nothing wrong. Rather it is about trying to give credit where credit is due and challenging yourself in hard situations to balance negative with positive, responsibility with forgiveness, and disdain with closeness, even in the face of imperfection.

TACTIC #76
COMPLEMENT, NOT COMPLETE

On Facebook the other day, I saw this funny meme. It said something like, "Cinderella was looking for a fancy dress and a night off; she wasn't actually looking for a prince." On TV, in the movies, and in fairy tales, we are continually bombarded by perfect relationships with idealized others, and the suggestion is that you aren't a complete person until you have a "better half."

This idea that you are somehow incomplete is incorrect. You do not need a partnership to make you your best self. In fact, you are unlikely to attract a person worthy of a long-term partnership if you feel incomplete or uncertain of yourself, if you're not rocking your strengths because you don't know what they are, or if you're not aware of your weaknesses and able to work around them.

It is a funny paradox, so common that it can seem cliché, but I see it all the time in my practice. As soon as someone stops striving for a relationship and starts working on his or her own issues, dating prospects suddenly and strangely radically improve. Here is when you meet Mr. or Ms. Right: when you stop looking outward, focus on improving yourself and your life, and get clear about who you are and what you have to offer to a relationship.

You are looking for someone to complement you in a relationship. You are looking to complement someone in a relationship. And I don't mean compliment, like telling someone he's wearing cool shoes. No, this is "complement" in the sense that you bring out the best in each other. Your strengths help mitigate their weaknesses and vice versa.

It is a winning combination for you both, where the sum is greater than the parts. This is not a situation where one person is carrying the other, but one where the couple carries the relationship.

First work on yourself, then look for that perfect match. Complement, not complete.

APPLY THIS: Take a minute and write down your top character traits. Are you funny, a great cook, organized, super social, or an expert outdoorsman? What do you bring to a partnership? These are the things you have to offer. Now take a minute and ask yourself what you'd enjoy your future mate to bring that would complement your strengths and work around your weaker points? This means it also helps to be honest (not dramatically critical or optimistically delusional) about your weaknesses.

For example, a friend of mine is a self-acknowledged terrible cook. However, she is a terrific adventurer and incredible traveler. When she is dating, she is looking for someone who wants to travel the world with her but also knows how to cook, is open to trying new restaurants, or is at the very least excellent at collecting takeout menus. This is travel and fine cuisine complementing each other.

TACTIC #77
THE EXCRUCIATING TRUTH ABOUT FREE WILL

Quick, what do these complaints have in common?

"I wish my daughter would take better care of herself."
"If only my son would stop using drugs."
"Why on earth does he keep putting up with her? They are a terrible match."
"Can't she see he's no good for her? They are a terrible match."

Here's the common thread between these complaints: People can use their free will to their detriment. Repeatedly. Let me say it another way. One of the most excruciating of our human experiences is watching someone you love use their free will to their detriment, on purpose, over and over.

As a psychologist, I am privy to people's issues, secrets, and patterns. One of the most painful things that a client brings in is his/her distress *about someone else's choices.* People agonize over their loved one's poor choices. They particularly suffer when they are watching someone they love make a bad choice, time after time, without seeming to learn from the consequences of their bad behavior. It is the absolute worst for people when their loved one *knows* they are behaving badly but get pulled back into the same horrible stuff again and again. It is a terrible feeling to stand helpless while those you care about make crummy choices. My clients beg for relief on this one. They ask me

Chapter 8: Enhance Relationships

how I can help them help their partner/child/friend/boss/co-worker/neighbor behave better.

My counsel on this one is not my favorite to dispense. You can't make anyone change; people only change of their own volition. You can instruct and lead by example, ask, demand, and even beg and plead, but people only change when they are ready to do so. They don't change a moment before they are ready to change. Not even if you *really* want them to. Lousy, right?

APPLY THIS: Your job is to accept the unpleasant life truth that people can use their free will in ways that are directly harmful to themselves and others, on purpose, consistently, over lots and lots of time. The translation here? People can behave badly, even when you don't want them to. Your job is to assess your role in the person's life and assist where you can, but otherwise, accept that their life choices are just that. Their life choices. Once you accept this fact, you can get some space from trying to bully, cajole, and otherwise manipulate someone into behaving better. It takes a lot of stress off when you understand where your limits are and where someone else's stuff begins. I didn't say it was very much fun, but it does help to get real about what is yours and what isn't. Oh, and please. Take a moment to examine where you are exercising your own free will. Hopefully, it isn't to your detriment. If it is, use that same free will to get yourself moving in a better direction.

TACTIC #78
THE JOY OF WIN-WIN
* A GOING DEEPER TIP

IN CONVERSATION, WITH everyone from your significant other to your child's teacher to the guy at the gas station, there are four main outcomes of any transaction.

From worst to best, here are the top four results of just about any interpersonal interaction:

1. Lose-Lose. Now, this is an outcome to be avoided. This outcome means no one walks away with what they wanted, and everyone is left holding the losing end of the stick. For example, you get into a fight with someone, say horrible things you can't take back; they do too, and everyone walks away feeling awful, mad, unsatisfied, unhappy, and wanting to break someone's kneecaps. No one wins, everyone loses, and the outcome is one big bummer.

2. Neutral. This outcome typically relates to the mundane. This is checking out in the grocery store and just having a transaction without active interaction. No smile, no knowledge, no understanding of the other person. Nothing negative, just a neutral transaction with nothing significant gained or lost on either side. Not every conversation with your Safeway clerk needs to be an exchange of witty or generous banter; it's to be expected that some interactions remain mundane.

But "neutral" can feel increasingly unsatisfying over time and is certainly unsatisfying if it's your primary outcome in interactions with your loved ones.

3. Win-Lose. This, interestingly, is often what people are after without acknowledging it to themselves or to the person with whom they are dealing. These are the situations where one person has an agenda to force through, and he or she walks away feeling victorious, leaving the other person feeling disconcerted, bullied, annoyed. One person wins; the other must lose. Now this can be deliberate (the power-hungry co-worker who loves throwing people under the bus) or inadvertent (your spouse eats the last of the chocolate, guessing you had some extra stashed away). Regardless of the thrill of a cheap victory now and then, this isn't the most elegant dynamic upon which to build your life.

4. Win-Win. The king of the interaction outcomes. Everyone walks away from the interaction feeling good. This is the gold standard, the one to strive for. It's mutually beneficial and helpful in both the long and short term. This often requires some understanding, good listening, a commitment to hearing and respecting both your own and other's desires. This outcome isn't always the easiest to achieve, but it is the best outcome because it encompasses mutually beneficial transactions in conversation or interaction.

Your goal is to try to keep in mind these four outcomes in your daily dealings with people. Can you challenge yourself to move them a level or two up the scale to win-win? You will feel better both in the moment and in the long run.

CHAPTER 9:
DE-STRESS

TACTIC #79
CHOOSE HEALTH

ONE QUESTION I always ask in my first meeting with a client is how they are doing with taking care of their basic physical health. I want to know how their diet and nutrition are, how often and what they do for exercise. I wonder how many hours they work and if they let themselves take breaks during the day. Often, these questions are the first place we start. Why do I start here? Because proper physical care fuels mental health functioning.

Regular physical self-care can help decrease and even eliminate some of the tricky negative mental messages that we feed ourselves. Often folks who are feeling down or struggling with anxiety stop caring for themselves, eat poorly, don't exercise, and fail to pay attention to their physical health. They isolate themselves from others and get stuck and closed in their own awful feeling world. Returning to basic self-care challenges those negative thinking patterns and helps lighten bad feelings, both by boosting good neurochemicals in your brain and reminding yourself that you are worthy and deserving of your own kindness. These positive patterns then build on each other and make you feel better over time.

Choosing health is even more important now than ever before as we are living in an increasingly toxic world. We are exposed to an incredible array of chemicals, air pollutants, genetically modified organisms, and water impurities. On top of that, most of the food available in a typical commercial grocery store is more of a combination of chemicals, super sweetened additives, and chemical dyes than anything resembling real food. All these things conspire to make us overweight, sluggish, increasingly allergic, hormonally chaotic, and foggy in our thinking. Sounds awful, right?

APPLY THIS: Choose health and combat the negative side effects of our modern world by eating real foods, minimizing sugar and junk foods, and making regular exercise a systemic part of your life. Set aside time in your schedule to work out, schedule time in your week to prepare healthy meals, take breaks during your day to attend to your self-care. Paradoxically, the time you spend taking care of yourself will fuel your productivity and performance, giving you more energy and allowing you to be more productive, attentive, and sharp. Start right now by choosing real food over processed, parking farther away and walking a few minutes, getting outside, or setting a date with a friend for a workout.

TACTIC #80
GET FRESH MORE OFTEN

WE HUMANS DO well when we are connected to a force in life larger than ourselves. Exposure to forces larger than ourselves helps us be less selfish, more aware of our interconnections, and get a nice rest from our own repetitive problems. It is an incredible opportunity to separate from our own tiny worlds, from the dynamics that can feel so oppressive and all-consuming, as we connect with something larger and more mysterious than our immediate personal concerns.

Now, religion and faith, of course, can serve some of this purpose, and I always encourage my spiritually inclined clients to pursue that avenue in their lives. But the easiest and most readily available option is to simply get outside in nature. There is a lot of joy and aliveness to be had in the conscious connection to our natural world.

How often do you make getting outside a priority in your life? This doesn't have to be an immersion in the backcountry wilderness for a month at a time, although if that is your cup of tea, go for it. I am talking about getting out of the canned, recycled, inside air and letting the sun hit your face. Feel the wind. Breathe. Walk a little and move that body. Get out of your chair, move away from the electronics, and eat lunch in the courtyard at work. Live in a big city? No worries; just get to a rooftop and enjoy. No rooftops nearby? Hang out at the closest park/tree/flower shop, whatever. See if you make some outside time, even if it is for five or ten minutes, a priority every day. Don't save it up for vacations or the weekend warrior thing. Small, daily, deliberate connection with nature can be even more beneficial than the occasional eight-hour hike when you happen to have the day free.

Chapter 9: De-Stress

APPLY THIS: How many small ways can you think of right now to increase your "fresh air" time? As I write, I have my window thrown wide open. Could you open a window? I wonder how many flowers you might see on a walk near your office. What harm could there be in a brief stroll after dinner? What about taking a break by getting outside and letting the sun kiss your face for a minute? Try it today, try it daily; I think you'll like it.

TACTIC #81
DO LESS

FEELING OVEREXTENDED? Do you have every minute planned? Do you work all week and then ferry your kids each night to a different activity? Never feel like you can get a rest? Carry your phone everywhere, even on vacation? All these obligations are crushing you. It's time to set some limits.

Let's take stock of your time. Take out a piece of paper and write down a typical week's schedule for yourself. How do you spend your time? Now, for the couch potatoes reading this who are under-scheduled, you may need to get out there and say yes to some things. For the rest of us, my guess is that your schedule is so tightly packed a sardine couldn't squeeze in there. List the obligations you are signed up for. Work, family, soccer, that board you volunteer for, long conversations with your needy friend, laundry, cleaning—you get the picture.

Now sort through your list. Of the things on the list, what do you love? What do you resent or dread doing each week? Think through why you do it anyway. Is it guilt? A sense of duty? Or is it something like the laundry, which needs to get done but isn't your favorite? Take a peek at the things you don't enjoy, and let's see what you can knock off of that column. Anything you can politely decline? Do less of? Schedule less frequently? Set better limits and boundaries on? Start with the stuff you despise. Even the laundry, which of course is necessary, can be less of a pain by doing it more efficiently, buying clothes that don't need to be ironed, etc.

Not doing what you love because of a crushing load of obligations? Sometimes, this is just life. For example, I know many first-time parents who are shocked at the differences in their lives before and after the baby arrives. Flexing with reality is important here.

I bring this up because we are often on autopilot with being agreeable, saying "Yes, sure." when what we actually mean is "No, dear God, please, no." Time to gear up and start being clear from the beginning of each new request for your time and attention. If you don't know or aren't sure what your answer should be, say, "Let me check; I will get back to you." Then look through your schedule and decide (realistically) if you have the emotional and physical room in your life to say "Yes." It is incredibly freeing to make choices about how you spend your time rather than feeling obligated to do it all.

APPLY THIS: Commit to writing out your list of tasks, obligations, roles, and assignments. Now scroll through the list and see what you can do less of. Anything you can assign to someone else? Could you hire someone to help? Can you just say no, or lessen your obligation somehow? Look through the list and figure out how to do less of what you don't love on a regular basis.

TACTIC #82
SYSTEMS ARE YOUR FRIEND

ONE OF THE great paradoxes in life is the amazing pattern I see that scheduling increases flexibility. I know, it sounds backward, right? Scheduling *increases* flexibility. Purposeful systems of designed activity help you feel less constrained, less limited. Weird, huh? Why does it work? Well, our brains are set up to reward us for doing things the same way, repeatedly. The trick is to deliberately design your brain pathways, choosing the way you want things set up, versus letting your mindless, unconscious habits run the show.

Okay, here goes. Look around your life and see what systems you already have in place. Do you always take the same route to work? Get up around the same time each day? How about your coffee habit? My guess is that you drink the same number of cups, from the same place, at about the same time. These are examples of systems you are already using. Which systems serve you well and which systems not so much? How about your bedtime? TV watching? Tendency to get cranky in boring work meetings? All are systems of reaction, using those brain pathways that prefer to do the same thing every time.

Looking at the habits you have gives you good information about what works well and what is not so helpful in your life. Then you can start designing systems and habits that work better for you. This will take some practice and is especially hard in the first few weeks you are trying to do things differently, but once you get over the initial hump, you can create new systems in your life that help you better. Then your life will become the product of the new habits you have chosen, an incredibly rewarding experience well worth the initial disruption.

Check out your life and identify what systems you want to add.

Want to work out four days a week? Schedule them in. Want to eat healthier? Schedule a time each week to shop and prep food, then schedule a time to put together your food for the day and eat it. Want to watch less TV and read more? Write in times to choose reading and shut off the TV.

APPLY THIS: To enjoy the freedom and flexibility healthy, positive habits can bring to your life, you need to do them on purpose—I promise they won't create themselves. Identify what you want more of and quantify it. Clarify what system you are looking for and specify how often, how much, when, where, and with whom. Then put it in your schedule. Start the day you think of it (change happens better today than tomorrow) and repeat it over the next month or so. Systematize your desired behaviors and see how it helps.

TACTIC #83
HOW'S YOUR SLEEP?

INCREASING RESEARCH ON sleep suggests it is one of the most critical building blocks to good mental and physical health. In addition, healthy sleep is related to maintaining a healthy weight, increases cognitive functioning and processing, and improves your mood. One of the first symptoms of declining mood and mental function is trouble with sleep, both falling asleep and staying asleep. One of the most annoying side effects of medication, hormone changes, stress, or a super crummy day, is trouble sleeping. Reports of trouble with insomnia and sleep are increasing at rapid rates and seem to reflect our high levels of stress, difficulty with systemic self-care, and trouble with overuse of substances.

So what is a sleepy guy or gal to do? Well, improving sleep hygiene is your first step. Sleep hygiene refers to the things we do around sleep, how we set ourselves up for a good night's sleep and what our environment is that we sleep in.

First things first. What time are you typically going to bed, and what time do you typically wake up? Are you generally logging less than seven hours? Going to bed after midnight? Start there by gradually pushing back your bedtime by fifteen minutes a night until you can naturally and easily fall asleep at a reasonable time and have seven to eight hours a night set aside for sleep.

Next, let's look at your sleep environment. Try eliminating electronics in your bedroom (I know, I know, that plasma looks so sweet on your wall) and limit your use of electronics after about 8:00 p.m., reserving your bedroom only for sleep or sex. Decrease clutter; make it a clean, calm environment. Dim the lights at least thirty minutes before you go to bed, or practice soothing rituals like making a glass of warm milk or a cup of herbal tea or taking a bath before bedtime.

Try hard to make your bedtime about the same time each night and your waking time similar, even on the weekends. This helps keep the rhythm in your mind and body so that sleep is consistent.

APPLY THIS: Enjoy the benefits of healthy sleep by improving your sleep environment and sleeping patterns. Try to have about the same bedtime each night. Do soothing, non-activating activities before bed. Keep work out of your bedroom. Keep your room cool and dark. Set yourself up for good sleep.

TACTIC #84
GO SHOPPING WITH FEEDBACK—BUY ONLY WHAT FITS

ARE YOU SENSITIVE when it comes to feedback? Do you find yourself believing everything someone says and frantically trying to change yourself? Or are you the type who resists hearing what someone says, gets defensive, and wants everything to be someone else's fault? In both cases, there tends to be an issue with hearing and acting on feedback, either negative or positive. It can be stressful to hear feedback, especially when someone is suggesting you have done something wrong, hurt their feelings, or aren't performing well.

One of the ideas I often talk to my clients about is the concept of going shopping with feedback. For those of you out there who hate to shop, think of this as the least painful shopping trip ever. Love to shop? Awesome. You and this tip will be good friends.

The concept here is to "try on" the feedback you are getting and see what fits. Consider the feedback as calmly and objectively as possible. Does it actually fit? Anything about it true? Does anything seem spot-on? Anything you already know about yourself? Great, then these are the things to act on, to relish (for the positive feedback), or admit and/or change (for those not-so-great comments).

Maybe the feedback fits in certain areas but not the entire garment. Does it feel too harshly negative or not quite accurate somehow? Okay, then this feedback offers something to consider and see if there is a kernel of truth that needs to be addressed. Is there some aspect that doesn't make any sense? You can certainly get more information about it.

Sometimes the person giving you the feedback may be talking about themselves or are so mad they will say anything negative or so enamored they will say anything nice, in which case you can decide that this feedback doesn't fit you.

This technique gives you permission to separate yourself a little bit from the commentary, examine it to determine what aspects, if any, deserve attention. This is about you being a little more thoughtful and objective, resisting our natural human urge to bask in praise or shrink from criticism. Approaching it from the shopping perspective helps you make more reasoned choices about how much you want to take on of the feedback and what to say/do with the person who delivered the information.

APPLY THIS: "Try on" the feedback you are receiving, positive or negative, and see how you like it. Imagine yourself examining each piece of feedback as you would some item for which you are shopping. Is it the right size? Fit your lifestyle and vision of yourself? Don't like it, but it still fits? Okay then, time to make some changes for yourself. Doesn't fit or barely makes sense? Seek more information if you feel like it can help your future, file it in your mind, and then walk away. It helps you gain clarity, identify action steps, and feel less stressed and overwhelmed when you apply this approach to feedback.

TACTIC #85
ACCEPT MORE (TRAFFIC, LINES, DELAYS)

I WAS READING AN article a while back (like six years ago, which is a bummer because I now have no idea where I encountered this) that talked about the concept of using life's minor hardships as opportunities to slow down and appreciate the moment. I'm pretty sure it was in a magazine about mindfulness because I dubbed this technique "Buddhist Lessons in Patience" and have been using it ever since. Now you certainly don't need to be a Buddhist to enjoy the technique, so let's re-name it "Lessons in Patience," or LIP for short.

What is an example of a LIP? How about that accident that is making you late for work? Or the person down the hall at work who ate your lunch today? You need to get something done and there is a line out the door when you need it to be quick? The elevator is broken and today is the day you have a huge load of stuff to bring up four flights of stairs? Feel free to insert any example that riles you up, makes you feel irritated, and generally exasperates you. Notice here that we are talking about the little irritations in life, not huge scary things that need a little more attention. These are the types of relatively harmless but aggravating incidents that can seduce us into a certain level of martyred drama in that moment, but if we slow down and breathe, we can act with intention, thereby gaining some valuable potential happiness points in mindfulness and compassion. Here are some suggestions about how to turn irritation into a Lesson In Patience.

Chapter 9: De-Stress

APPLY THIS: Your first step here is to recognize that this annoying situation is an opportunity to experience a LIP by accepting more and resisting less. Think to yourself, *ahh, I am feeling irritated because of (fill in the annoying situation here), this is an opportunity to see this as a Lesson in Patience.* Then you can breathe deeply, in through your nose and out through your mouth. You can deliberately relax your shoulders, wiggle your body until you feel less tense. Try slowing down your irritated mind by thinking (and breathing while thinking) that this is something you can handle. You will make it through just fine. Things will turn out okay; this is just a minor irritation, nothing to get so worked up about. Accept the interference in your plan. Imagine something positive, remember your last great conversation, recall a funny scene from a book or movie. Settle yourself down and enjoy the moment where you have been forced to increase patience, slow down and smile, despite the problem. Repeatedly reassure yourself. Accept the moment even though it isn't what you hoped for.

TACTIC #86
IMPROVE YOUR INTERNAL MOOD BY MANAGING YOUR EXTERNAL ENVIRONMENT

FEELING LIKE YOU can't quite catch up with your life? Does it seem like everything is a mess all around you? Confused about what step to take next? Sometimes our internal environments are quite a mess. We struggle with negative thoughts and are swamped with complaints and judgments about ourselves and others. Maybe we have a tremendous amount of scattered thinking and can't seem to focus on anything long enough to get it done, or we have so many ideas swarming around we can't figure out what to prioritize.

One of the things I almost always ask my clients is how their houses, cars, desks, and offices look. Most of the time, when someone is struggling with their thoughts or emotions (internal environment), they will report that their external environment (house, car, desk, or room) is mirroring their internal issues. It is common for someone who is depressed to tell me that their apartment is dark, they have the shades drawn, and aren't letting in any light. The person who is scattered and unfocused will describe a home or office that is piled high with partially completed projects. The anxious person will tell me that they have too much stuff and know they need to let go of things but can't make themselves take that first step and cull through their belongings.

Strangely, sometimes the solution to a messy internal environment is to clean things up in our external environment. Look around your house, desk, office, car, or any other space you inhabit. What is your space saying about you? Do you notice any similarities between your internal and external environments? Do yourself a favor and try cleaning up that external environment and see what effect it makes on your internal one.

APPLY ONE OF THESE SOLUTIONS:

Feeling stuck? Clean your car, counters, junk drawer(s), or something else you have let get messy.

Feeling down and gloomy? Open your shades and let in some light. Clean and air out your house. Bring in a plant that requires your love, attention, and care.

Feeling anxious and overwhelmed? Clean up those piles that have been sitting there forever. Start with one area, like a closet, and get rid of anything you have been saving and not using. If the closet seems too big, start with an area of one square foot. If it isn't useful, beautiful, or important in some way, let it go. By tackling one square foot a day, you can have a cleaner, calmer environment in short order.

Constantly unfocused and scattered? Organize your desk, pay your bills, get a system to deal with your mail or other paperwork. Pick up one pile and get it put away, then tackle the next pile.

Don't try to force a change in your internal environment, just see if cleaning up your external environment naturally makes a shift in your thoughts or feelings.

TACTIC #87
TIME BLOCKING

IN THE FIFTH grade, I had the fortunate experience of having a great teacher. Miss Leigh was smart, fair, and cared about her students. She could help you learn hard things and make them seem easy. Most importantly, she could make you feel special without playing favorites. She gave me nice feedback overall and motivated me to become a better student. In giving me feedback on one report card, she let me (and my parents) know that I needed to improve my time management skills. I guess I had lots of ideas but wasn't so good at getting them done on time. Because I still have lots of ideas and limited time, I turn to the experts for advice on how to better manage my time.

Now you may ask why a tip on time management is included in the managing stress section of this book. Easy. If you aren't managing your time well, it increases stress. Typically, folks who struggle in this arena feel pressure with deadlines, may leave things until the last minute (procrastination = more pressure), or have a hard time prioritizing their tasks, so they end up always feeling behind. Stressful.

How do you manage your time better, anyway? Is it possible to do so and make levels of stress and exhaustion come down? One of the most helpful ideas I have found in all my research on the subject relates to the concept of honoring our natural circadian rhythms in our bodies and using those natural ebbs and flows of energy to drive our productivity. This idea of rhythms suggests that we alternate between periods of work/rigor and relaxation/rest. The suggestion here is to block off periods of work and then schedule time for rest and renewal.

Yes, yes. I can hear some of you howling that you have too much work to do to indulge in rest. Relaxation is for lazy people, not productive machines like yourself. Well, I must disagree. Rest is critical for success, for everyone, even you. Trust me.

APPLY THIS: Divide your time into periods of fifty minutes or so of focused work, preferably on a task-oriented goal, resisting the urge to multitask a million things at once. At the end of the fifty minutes, take a ten-minute break. During your break, change your body position as it helps reset your brain and keeps you fresh when you reconnect with your work again. For example, if you have been at your computer, get up and walk. If you have been on the phone, make sure to do something that releases your neck and shoulders. Standing on the job? Okay, then try to sit on your break. Every couple of hours, take a slightly longer break and get a snack and hydrate. Then get back to the fifty-minute work blocks and ten-minute breaks.

If this doesn't work in your schedule, adapt it to what makes the most sense for your work. Only have time for a two-minute break? Okay, breathe, stretch, change positions, and then get back to it. Focus on deliberately creating alternating periods of rest and rigor, using your natural circadian rhythms to guide you into what makes the most sense for your body and your work.

SELF-HELP ON THE GO

TACTIC #88
BRICK WALLS IN THE SAND
*A GOING DEEPER TIP

I was lucky enough to grow up (mostly) in Virginia Beach, Virginia. Where we lived was about eight minutes from the intersection of the Atlantic Ocean and the Chesapeake Bay. At this intersection, there happens to be a military base, and they do all sorts of live ordinance (read: grenades) training on this base. They aren't too keen on folks walking on their property, and they put up a fence on the beach where the ocean and the bay meet. So, while you could go down to the ocean and take a nice, long walk, at the end of the beach you would run into a wall and have to walk back. No questions asked. You needed to accept that limit and turn around. Period.

I was thinking one day about the expression "drawing lines in the sand." My experience with lines in the sand, both on a beach and when applying the metaphor to the rest of life, is that lines drawn in the sand are easily changed. Before you know it, you can find yourself a mile away from your original intention because you kept moving the boundary for yourself. It made me think about that wall in the sand at the end of the beach, and I thought, *why not create "walls in the sand"?* Lines that can't be crossed. Values that can't be breached because you have decided beforehand that they are non-negotiable and can't be messed with. Thinking beforehand means less stress in the moment when big choices come your way.

I started using this idea with teenagers to help them make decisions *early* about what their values were and creating a strong visualization of a "wall in the sand" about these values, so they would be less likely to bend under peer pressure. Then I extended this work to adults, and they also found it helpful. This concept of deciding before you even start where your end is and what lines you won't cross helps you make better decisions regardless of your age.

What are some examples of brick walls in the sand?

1. Never start smoking cigarettes, ever. Don't even try that first "harmless" one.

2. Wait until you are an adult to have sex. That means you can tell your boyfriend/girlfriend that it isn't even something on the table. (Of course, this is a complex conversation since "adult" means sixteen years old to some, eighteen to others, and don't even get me started on the definition of sex.) All these things are put into the "wall" construction and are unique to each person.

3. Say no to all the hard drugs. Every time, every situation, forever.

4. Only date people who are unattached. Your married professor? Pass on him. Your buddy's on-again and off-again girlfriend? Pass on her too.

5. Don't steal from your workplace, not even the pencils or paperclips.

You get the idea. Some of this is basic morality stuff; some is a little more complex. But overall, the idea of deciding before you have to decide is powerful and decreases stress because you already have your answer prepared. What brick walls might you enjoy building in your life?

CHAPTER 10:
LIVE THE LIFE YOU WANT

TACTIC #89
THOUGHTS BECOME THINGS

THE OTHER DAY, I was talking to a client who was feeling discouraged. She was paying almost complete attention to a problem in her world. New job, in over her head, she was beating herself up and feeling inadequate. She was bombarded with these difficult thoughts and had trouble giving herself credit for pretty much anything else. And, coincidently, the more she was focused on not doing well at her new job, the more mistakes she seemed to be making, which made her panic even more.

We started talking about how thoughts become things. What I mean by this is that what we focus on tends to grow in both scope and intensity. And we are often misled by our thinking. It is true that nearly 100 percent of the time, we are experiencing positive, negative, and neutral input. However, we are often only highlighting one aspect of that input. And our brains seem to be particularly good at highlighting those negatives. Once highlighted, these thoughts get bigger and louder and more developed, encouraging us to focus on them more. Scope (how big they are) and intensity (how much we feel them) both grow under these conditions.

Challenging yourself to span out from the narrow spotlight on the negative tends to give us more perspective. Once we can see the entirety of what is truly going on, then we can better see options for success. And we can feel more balanced and less overwhelmed.

TRY THIS: Imagine you are in the audience of a play and focusing only on one small area of the stage with a spotlight. Now bring up the house lights and let your vision focus on the breadth of things on the stage. Instead of that one spotlight, notice the varied things to look at on that stage. Use this same technique with your thoughts. Ask yourself where you have too narrow of a focus and bring up the lights so to speak on the rest of the inputs you have been ignoring. Let the scope and intensity of your thoughts grow on thoughts that you actively want to examine, rather than being bullied around only by the negative thoughts. See how this gives you more choice and control about how to decide on your next best move?

TACTIC #90
READY, SET, ACTION

EVER HEARD ABOUT the "Law of Attraction" where you think your way into success? Well, the theory forgets to mention that it is not enough (most of the time) to think about what you want. Even if you get specific, there is another step to take, especially for those bigger goals. You must also take *action* toward your ideal. Ever heard the old joke about asking God to win the lottery? It goes like this: When you finally get to heaven and never won, you ask God, "Why didn't I win the lottery? I asked and asked, and you never came through; why not?" To which God replies, "Sweetie. You have to buy a ticket."

How do we apply this in real life? Build on the idea from the last tip that thoughts become things. Be clear about what you want and then take action to get what it is you are looking for. It is in this wonderful combination that good things happen. Looking for a partner? First, identify what characteristics you are looking for and not looking for. (Tip #69 teaches you about this.)

Now, the action: It is highly unlikely you will attract this next wonderful mate by sitting at home, socializing only with people you already know, and refusing to meet new people. Time to take a risk, get out there, and date. The same principles apply if it is something super small, like wishing for a great parking spot—you can't just wish for it. You still have to drive around.

Use the same concept for the *really* challenging stuff, like professional success. You'll need to get the appropriate training, work hard, network, and apply yourself conscientiously to get that dream job. This also works with less tangible goals like increased inner peace (you'll need to start practicing the things which will lead you there)

Chapter 10: Live The Life You Want

or improved relationships (imagine them, so you can feel the feelings associated, then take action to learn and apply better communication skills). Chapter 6, on communication, could help you with these goals.

APPLY THIS: After you have identified what it is that you want and have made your list or vision board (where you put together pictures and quotes about what you want all on one posterboard), take the next move and identify action steps to get you closer to getting what you want. Map out what options you have, large and small, to propel yourself into achieving your goal. Talk about your goal with others and get their feedback about possible action steps. Interview someone who already has what you want and ask them how they got there. Do your research. Above all, act.

TACTIC #91
GET SMART

One of the easiest traps to get into is to think about something and never complete the goal. Ever made a New Year's resolution that only lasted a day or two? Ever wanted to start a diet and then found yourself stopping for fast food by 10:00 a.m.? I think we've all been there. The trick is to give your goal a little boost so you can cross that gap between thinking and doing. A terrific way to act toward your goals is to SMART your goal. This is a classic neurolinguistic programming technique that can help you cross that bridge from idea to implementation.

SMART is: S = specific, M = measurable, A = actionable, R = realistic, and T = time based.

Here's a goal I bet many of us have entertained: I'd like to win a million dollars. This is both specific and measurable and even sort of actionable since I can buy lotto tickets. However, it falls apart in the realistic (seen those lotto odds lately?) and time-based (no control over those odds so I can't set a timeline) sections.

Let's take another common goal, one we can certainly make SMART. Many of my clients have partially finished their college degrees. To a person (male, female, minority, non-minority, financially well off, struggling with money), if this is something they truly wanted, they *all* express frustration that they haven't completed their education. In addition, many of them are finding they are trapped in crappy jobs they are afraid to leave due to their lack of a degree. Here is where a SMART goal can help tremendously:

Goal: I would like to finish my college degree.

Chapter 10: Live The Life You Want

Specific: Bachelor's degree in (pick your favorite major here).

Measurable: Meet with a college advisor at (put your favorite educational institution here). I need 120 credits to graduate, with sixty in my major. They will transfer in forty credits toward general classes and twenty toward my major. Fantastic, I have a head start.

Actionable: Complete my application and get accepted as a transfer student. I need to complete my financial aid packet. Register to start the fall semester.

Realistic: Take night and weekend classes so my education doesn't compete with my job. I will speak with my employer so they are aware of two classes I will need to take during daytime hours. I have budgeted for this and am applying for scholarships too.

Time-Based: I will begin classes on August 15. I have a two-year timeframe for completion, which allows me enough time to work and still attend school.

 Next time you have a goal, either large or small, try to SMART it. Identify how you can make it specific, measurable, actionable, realistic, and time-based. Then start with the first action step and move on forward.

TACTIC #92
MOVE AWAY FROM MATERIALISM

IF YOU ARE a typical citizen in a developed country, then you are likely familiar with the rush toward acquiring material goods. If you are a US citizen (I think we may be the world's worst offenders), you are likely bombarded daily with ads on television, billboards, magazines, newspapers, and other media to spend money and acquire the next best thing. Just to add to the pressure, many things you spent good money on, say a computer, or a television, or a fancy cell phone, are now becoming obsolete almost before you are finished paying.

The interesting thing is, as we are pushed toward this material acquisition, we are being told with indirect and direct messages that acquiring new goods will increase our happiness. Now, this is fascinating since, despite the relentless messages to the contrary, money and happiness are not well connected. Even though most of us assume that money will solve our problems and make us more content and happier, this doesn't bear out in real life for most folks. If you look at the extreme end of things, like studying folks who have come into a huge sum of money, such as a major inheritance, there is a super interesting phenomenon afoot because many of them report a return to pre-winning happiness levels within a year of getting the money.

APPLY THIS: The answer here is to challenge yourself to buy in less to the messages by buying less. Resist the pressure to acquire material goods, remember that meaningful relationships, work, and activities *consistently and reliably* provide more satisfaction than material goods. Set up your life so you don't spend more than you make. Purchase less, regardless of your income level. Simplifying, acquiring less, and living within your means are all excellent ways to increase freedom in your life. And that freedom decreases stress and pressure and increases happiness.

TACTIC #93
BUDGETING CAN SET YOU FREE

WHILE WE ARE supposed to move away from materialism, we still have to live, and living, the last time I checked, is expensive. Herein lies the magic and wonder of budgeting. The act of budgeting allows one to get clear about what money is coming in and to get especially clear about what money is going out. Many of us avoid money talks, avoid thinking about money, and even avoid knowing what is going on with our money. Ever found yourself not opening the bills? Stopped checking your balances because you don't want to know the totals? Pretend you still have money since the credit card wasn't declined yet?

Budgeting isn't for the faint of heart, and it takes real courage both to look at and then deal with the realities of your money situation. Let's break this down step by step:

First, you need to accurately assess how much money is coming in. This number is what you have after taxes and insurance and all that jazz. How much money do you have available to spend?

Second, what are your bills each month, and when are they due? Do the math. Are you overspending (most Americans are), underspending (congratulations), or breaking even?

Finally, do the tough thing: cut out unnecessary expenses. Some are reasonably easy: chop off the extras on the cable bill, stop the subscription to the monthly online gaming site. Some are habits to break: make your own coffee in the morning, pack your own lunch, stop smoking (it's killing you, which is a waste of money), check out books from the library. Then there are the big ones; major behavior change is needed here: In tons of credit card debt? Put yourself on a cash-only basis. Medical bills or other lingering debts? Call and set up payment plans. Get a financial advisor to help you identify your personal blind spots in spending. Identify and make changes, large and small to move you toward greater financial independence and security.

APPLY THIS: Do this the old-fashioned way on a piece of paper, or get fancy and use a reputable online budgeting tool. First, get clear about what you have to work with each month. Then, list your monthly obligations and when they are due. List your debts, both how much you owe and how much you put toward them monthly. Are you paying on the premiums or are you paying interest? List your other expenses, the ones that don't necessarily come in bill form, like groceries, gas, clothes, eating out. Now compare the numbers. Once you subtract your bills, debt payments, and expenses, how much do you have leftover? Set up a monthly budget and stick to it.

TACTIC #94
HAVE A HOBBY

Just before I turned forty, I woke up one day and realized that middle age wasn't just approaching; it had arrived. As I took stock, I realized two major things. First, I felt frumpy and out of shape. Second, I realized that I was out of balance in my life. I was working much, much more than I was playing, and it showed in my body and my mood. I started working out with a trainer at my local rec center and ended up on a long and strange journey to adopt powerlifting as my hobby. A decade later, I am in better shape than I have been since I was in my twenties, and I feel strong instead of frumpy. But most of all, my work-play balance is, well, in better balance.

Balance is a term thrown around a lot these days. At the most basic level, it means your life has a healthy mixture of work and play, adventure and comfort, fresh and familiar, activity and downtime. Living a more balanced life creates a comfortable feeling inside and helps generate more even-keeled emotional functioning.

Now the hard part is achieving balance and still meeting your goals and responsibilities. This obviously gets exponentially more complex when you are trying to achieve multiple objectives at once. Anybody trying to be successful at work, healthy and fit, a terrific parent, good to your family, great friend, making money, and taking care of yourself, all at the same time? Me too.

It certainly can be difficult to play when you have so much to take care of. One solution is to have a hobby. Hobbies are an adult's playtime. If you check out the difference in the number of hours kids play versus adults, it is enough to make a grownup cry. Having a hobby increases balance, is playful, and helps you move away from life stressors while caring for your own needs.

APPLY THIS: Pick up a hobby. Not sure what hobby to go with? Well, one way is to remember some of the activities you loved as a kid and reintroduce them into your life. Maybe you want to build model cars again or join a softball league. Maybe you love to paint, so you can take lessons on Saturdays. It isn't so important what it is, or even how well you do it if it is something you love to do. Participating in activities you love increases joy, builds energy, and decreases stress, all of which can help you be a more patient parent, more creative worker, happier spouse, and a better friend. So, yes, you *do* have time.

TACTIC #95
GIVE BACK

ONE OF LIFE's great paradoxes is that as we feel worse, we tend to close ourselves off and give less to others. Recently, I had a client struggling with serious depression. He came in talking about how empty his life is and how nothing has any luster for him anymore. He was almost entirely focused on his problems, how bad his life is, how unappealing he is to others, and how he couldn't even remember how to feel joy.

This is, of course, a serious and complicated case, but one solution we discussed involved a commitment to volunteering several hours a week. Why volunteering? Well, the more internally focused we are, the more we tend to brood, feel dissatisfied, and pick away at ourselves. Certainly, some introspection is critical to our mental health and development, but over-focusing on ourselves, especially on our myriad faults, generally spirals us downward. An easy way to lift our spirits, put life in perspective, and improve our feelings about ourselves is to give to others.

Volunteering can partner with the previous suggestion to get involved in a hobby. Pick an activity that is near and dear to your heart. If you always adored horses but don't have the time/inclination/funding to have your own horse, work at a horse rescue. Love soccer? Coach a youth league team. Outdoorsy? Participate in a trail cleanup day at a nearby park. Volunteering can also help combat materialism (have your family give donations at the holidays instead of overspending on easily forgotten trinkets), build family time (have everyone, even the little people, help monthly at a food bank) and

Chapter 10: Live The Life You Want

increase your well-being as you add to the lives of others. (Ever seen the smile of a Special Olympics kid? Best thing ever.)

APPLY THIS: Look around your community and see what organizations might need some help. Challenge yourself to spend at least two hours a month volunteering. Think of a way you would like to give back, make a difference, be involved. Sign up and give it a try. I have seen everything from a one-hour stint at a local church to fostering animals for months at a time make a difference. Pick what makes sense to you and focus on something outside of your ordinary everyday world. I think you will be pleased with the results.

TACTIC #96

MEANINGFUL WORK IS A GREAT THING— FIND THAT CALLING
* A GOING DEEPER TIP

MANY YEARS AGO, when I was still in graduate school, I had a friend call me to obtain sympathy for her large tax bill. Now she had been working since college, was extremely talented, and in a field where she made loads of money. I, on the other hand, went to college and then kept going with school programs and nonprofit work, so I didn't have two pennies to rub together. However, I was working with cool kids when I wasn't in school. When she told me the total of her tax bill, I laughed and asked for sympathy myself because it turns out I had made, in an entire year, $36 more than she owed in taxes.

As I started complaining about my poverty level, she interrupted me and said, "Yes, but you love what you do; you get to help people and get to make a difference. I might be more comfortable financially, but I'm not helping others." And suddenly I felt very rich. (Note that soon after our conversation, she volunteered as a big sister and eventually changed jobs to one that suited her values and purpose better.)

One of the saddest statements I hear clients (and friends) make is that they hate their jobs. They talk about feeling trapped and limited and wake up each morning not feeling good about their work. A recent internet survey I read indicated that 87 percent of Americans dislike their jobs. How horrible. Sure, money is a means to an end, but we need a fair amount of it, and thus most of us work for a living. Most of us also need to work full-time, meaning a huge proportion of our waking hours are spent at the office, dealing with work-related items. For someone who hates their job, this means they are spending most of their life doing something they don't like. Yuck.

Choosing work that means something to you, makes a difference in the world, interests you, and/or is something you enjoy doing can make a considerable difference in your life. Imagine waking up in the morning and looking forward to your day. Think about enjoying your work so much it feels exciting to you, recharges you as you are doing it. An intriguing idea, isn't it? Sort of like combining a hobby and a career. It doesn't matter if your calling is in restaurant work, social work, fixing cars, doing hair, being a doctor or an engineer, pursue the path that lights your fire, holds your interest, and energizes you.

APPLY THIS: Spend some time imagining what your ideal career would look like. What field interests you the most? What are the elements of those jobs that grab your attention? Now research to find out the credentials you need to get into that field. Anything you need to do differently in your life? Sometimes clients of mine have had to move, go back to school, learn new skills, or get special training to do what they love. Start at the beginning by identifying what you want, and then take steps to move toward your ideal career. Good luck. I hope you get to love what you do for a living because you will then be rich in a truly exceptional way.

TACTIC #97
ALIGN YOUR VALUES, PRIORITIES, AND ACTIONS

This is a super interesting exercise: Let's identify what you *think* you prioritize and then compare it against how you choose to spend your time. Often there is a huge disparity between what we *believe* our top priorities to be and how we are spending our time.

A typical result looks like this:

Top Priorities:	Top Activities:
Family	Work
Being a good spouse	Chores
Friends	Paperwork
Health	TV
Helping others	Family

Looks a little off, right? It seems the activities column is missing some date nights, social time, and giving back. I wonder how this person could balance work and family a little better and how they might schedule some time for pleasure.

It can be incredibly helpful to better align your values, priorities, and actions. First, identify your core values: what is most important to you? What makes your life meaningful? Then strive to make your activities reflect these valued priorities. Maybe this means you will work less or work more efficiently, turn off the TV more, focus on healthy eating, or make chores less time-consuming. Maybe you will add in a lot more fun. The ideas and possibilities are limitless, and I promise that life will get way more interesting. And juicy.

TRY THIS: Identify the top five people/things/activities/values you hold dear and compare them to the top five ways you spend your time.

Priorities: Time:
1.   1.
2.   2.
3.   3.
4.   4.
5.   5.

As you compare the two lists, what gaps do you see? How can you better align your priorities and actual behaviors? Start today.

TACTIC #98
CHASIN' JOY

One of my clients came in and was struggling in his life, feeling like he used to be this lighthearted, easy-going guy, good at socializing, having fun, and being creative. He described himself now as a person who was working hard, providing for his family, and overwhelmed with responsibilities. He felt he had lost a large bit of the fun-loving, easy-going guy he used to enjoy being. In our conversations, we decided that he needed to return to "Chasin' Joy" (he's from the South, and I basically am too, so we decided the informal spelling was both perfect for the saying and honored our southern roots). So, Chasin' Joy became his homework assignment. Really and truly.

He was tasked to figure out how often he could find something to enjoy or laugh about. How many times in one week could he combine his regular life with joyful activities that brought a smile to his face and lightened the mood of those around him? Could he find something every day? What were his long-term goals for joy? Could he do something about those long-term goals in the present moment?

When was the last time you scheduled playtime for yourself? What joy are you chasing? The nifty thing about playtime is it is popular with almost everyone. You can include family, kids, friends, even co-workers to some degree. Chasin' Joy is an incredible way to make life more playful, enjoyable, and energizing. It shifts your focus from the daily grind to seeking out daily joys, large and small.

Chapter 10: Live The Life You Want

APPLY THIS: Invest in and commit to playtime in your life. It doesn't have to be time-consuming or expensive, but it should be a priority. Seek out small, medium, and large joys. Figure out ways to schedule in fun and lightheartedness. What might make you joyful today? Be sure to schedule it into your day. Enjoy that joy.

TACTIC #99
REPEAT AND REPAIR

All these tips are lovely ideas, but they only work if you implement them. Of course, some are easy to put into practice in the moment, others you need to think about and implement over time, but the common denominator is application. The thing that makes the application easier is tracking your progress. And the best way to track your progress is to both monitor and modify, repeating what works and repairing what doesn't.

This is about objectively identifying what is working and what isn't in those best-laid plans and making changes accordingly. This is valuable in arenas small and large. Here is an example: I had a client scheduled today who is chronically late, all the time, to everything. We started by monitoring the problem. In examining her lateness, she discovered two main issues. First, there was a fear of success (long-term therapy stuff to chew on). Second, there was a basic, easily remedied scheduling glitch: she doesn't leave herself enough drive time. Our longer-term plan is to work through the fear of success piece over time in therapy. But we started at that moment by concretely solving the drive time issue. The fix? She is going to give herself fifteen minutes above her estimated drive time, no matter where she goes.

APPLY THIS: Whether you are working on a micro-type of activity (like the lateness issue above) or a macro issue (how are you coming along in your spiritual development?), the approach is the same: Start by monitoring what is working and what isn't so well in your life. Then modify by repeating the positives (what's working) and repairing the negatives (what isn't working so well).

Keep track of your progress. What goes well? What causes failures? What did you think would make a difference and has? Anything that hasn't? Then, and this is the cool step, do *more* of what works and *less* of what doesn't. Monitor and modify. Repeat and repair. Over and over again. I wish you the best. You are worth it.

APPENDIX

ACKNOWLEDGMENTS

Years ago, my clients asked me to write this book. They wanted a shorter, easier-to-apply self-help book that would give them quick ideas about how to handle life's challenges in the moment. First and foremost, I want to acknowledge my fantastic clients over the past twenty years in private practice, and before that, in community mental health. It is truly an honor and a privilege to do the work I do and to work with people who bravely come in and share their stories and then dig in and make remarkable changes.

Thanks to Dr. Chris Sheldon for early assistance with the concept and initial chapters of this book. I appreciate your insight, guidance, and friendship over the past two decades. Fabulous author and speaker Mary LoVerde deserves thanks for encouraging me to get past my "very sh**ty first draft." Author and coach extraordinaire Brenda Abdilla has been a champion of mine both personally and professionally and has been an incredible source of wisdom, friendship, and inspiration.

My marvelous circle of friends, incredible family, wonderful husband, and delightful daughter deserve heartfelt thanks for believing in this project over a long, long time. Having healthy, happy relationships is pretty much the pivot point in my world. I love you guys!

ABOUT THE AUTHOR

Dr. Carrie runs a thriving therapy practice founded on the philosophy that no one is broken, but we all have important things we need to work on to improve our habits, communication, relationships, and daily functioning. She uses evidence-based treatments teaching acceptance and empowerment to help her clients effect change, treat trauma, manage anxiety, and live a more meaningful and enjoyable life. Dr. Carrie is hired to speak to groups, organizations, and businesses because she combines the latest developments in psychology with easy-to-implement strategies to improve performance and resiliency.

Dr. Carrie has been working in the therapy field for over twenty years. She became a psychologist because she realized her passion was helping people get unstuck and out of their own way. Her undergraduate degree is from the University of Virginia, her masters in counseling from the University of Denver, and her doctorate in psychology from the University of Northern Colorado. She has been a licensed psychologist since 2003.

On a personal note, Dr. Carrie is halfway through doing fifty hikes to celebrate turning fifty. Pretty much anytime she can, you will find her outside, with a friend if one is available, taking in the lovely Colorado scenery.

WORKS REFERENCED

1. Sonja Lyubomirsky, *The How of Happiness: A New Approach to Getting the Life You Want* (New York: Penguin, 2008).
2. Charles Darwin, *The Expression of the Emotions in Man and Animals* (London: John Murray, 1872).
3. Lyubomirsky, *The How of Happiness.*
4. Dr. Salvatore R Maddi and Deborah M. Khoshaba, *Resilience at Work: How to Succeed No Matter What Life Throws at You* (New York: Amacon Books, 2005).
5. Chuck Blakeman, "Why the f-word is the right response to everything", *Inc.*, May 19, 2015, https://www.inc.com/chuck-blakeman/why-the-f-word-is-the-right-response-in-every-circumstance-no-exceptions.html
6. Elisabeth Kubler-Ross, *On Death and Dying* (New York: Macmillan Publishing, 1969).
7. Russ Harris, *The Happiness Trap* (New York: Trumpeter Random House. 2008).
8. Jack Kornfield, *No Time Like the Present: Finding Freedom, Love, and Joy Right Where You Are* (New York: Atria Books, 2017).
9. James Baraz, "Awakening Joy: 10 Steps to a Happier Life," https://awakeningjoy.info/.
10. Gretchen Rubin, *The Happiness Project* (New York: Harper, 2009).
11. Douglas Stone, Bruce Patton, and Sheila Heen, *Difficult Conversations: How to Discuss What Matters Most* (New York: Penguin Books, 2010).
12. *Billy Madison*, directed by Tamra Davis, screenplay by Adam Sandler and Tim Herlihy (Universal City, CA: Universal Pictures, February 10, 1995).
13. Judith Viorst, *Alexander and the Terrible, Horrible, No Good, Very Bad Day* (New York: Atheneum Books for Young Readers, 1972).
14. Gary Chapman, *The Five Love Languages* (Chicago: Northfield Publishing, 2015).
15. John Gottman, *Why Marriages Succeed or Fail: What You Can Learn from the Breakthrough Research to Make Your Marriage Last* (New York: Simon & Schuster, 1994).